GLENCOE

Health

A Guide to Wellness

Student Workbook

 **Glencoe McGraw-Hill**

New York, New York   Columbus, Ohio   Woodland Hills, California   Peoria, Illinois

Glencoe/McGraw-Hill

A Division of The **McGraw·Hill** *Companies*

Printed in the United States of America.

Send all inquiries to :
Glencoe/McGraw-Hill
21600 Oxnard Street, Suite 500
Woodland Hills, California 91367

ISBN 0-02-651565-2 Student Workbook
ISBN 0-02-651566-0 Student Workbook Teacher's Annotated Edition

2 3 4 5 6 7 8 9   066   02 01 00 99

Table of Contents

UNIT 5   BODY SYSTEMS

UNIT 10   INJURY PREVENTION AND SAFETY

CHAPTER 1 Vocabulary

health	health literacy	culture
wellness	heredity	risk factors
lifestyle factors	environment	values
prevention	peers	abstinence
health education		

Directions ➤ A number of different relationships exist among words and phrases and the ideas they represent.

- A *hierarchical relationship* is a relationship in which one word is higher in rank than another. Examples: *boss → employee; teacher → student.*
- A *cause-effect relationship* is a relationship in which a condition or event represented by one word is a possible cause of a condition or event represented by another. Examples: *rain → wet; accident → injury.*
- A *parallel relationship* is a relationship in which two or more words share an equivalent status. Examples: *brother → sister; apple → orange.*

Use the information on word relationships to answer the questions that follow.

1. Explain the cause-effect relationship between the terms *wellness* and *health education.*

_____

_____

2. Identify another term from the list above that has a cause-effect relationship with health education. Explain that relationship.

_____

_____

3. Self-directed learner, a phrase from the chapter, has a hierarchical relationship with one of the terms in the list above. Identify that term. Name two other phrases that have the same relationship with the term identified in the list.

_____

_____

_____

4. In what way might the terms heredity and environment be said to exhibit a parallel relationship?

_____

_____

5. Write an original sentence that shows a parallel relationship between the terms prevention and abstinence.

_____

_____

ACTIVITY **1** Applying Health Skills

| attitude | health-literate | wellness |
| health education | lifestyle factor | prevention |

A Nose for News

Directions ➤ Below are excerpts from newspaper articles, each with a health theme. In the space following each excerpt, write the key health concept or concepts from the box above to which the excerpt relates. Include a brief paragraph explaining the relationship.

1. ***WOMAN LOSES LAWSUIT AGAINST TOBACCO COMPANY***

MIDLAND CITY—After only two hours of deliberation, the jury today returned a judgment in favor of the defendant, P&J Tobacco Company, and against the plaintiff, Gladys Wilcox, in a $10,000,000 civil case. According to one juror, a major factor in the jury's decision was the testimony of Ms. Wilcox, a long-time smoker who filed suit against P&J last year after developing lung cancer. "Ms. Wilcox's testimony revealed that she failed to keep abreast of current available information linking tobacco use to cancer and several other diseases," the juror told reporters.

Key concept(s): _____

Explanation: _____

_____

_____

_____

_____

2. ***NOBEL PRIZE IN MEDICINE AWARDED TO LOCAL SCIENTIST***

Special to the Gainesburg Tribune

STOCKHOLM—Last night, Dr. Jamal Wilson was awarded the Nobel Prize in Medicine for his discovery of a cure for Rivington's disease, an affliction common among people who are overweight. A lifetime resident of Gainesburg, Dr. Wilson humbly commented in his acceptance speech that "discoveries such as mine are not enough. It is up to every individual to take measures to avoid becoming overweight in the first place." Noting that one-third of all adults in the United States are clinically obese, Dr. Wilson went on to add that "another obstacle we must overcome is the refusal of many Americans to believe in the health benefits of an eating style high in fiber and low in fat and cholesterol."

Key concept(s): _____

Explanation: _____

_____

_____

_____

_____

ACTIVITY **2** **Applying Health Skills**

A Day in the Life

Directions ➤ In the chapter you were asked to imagine that the story of your health had been made into a video. The passage that follows depicts a scene from the health video of a teen named Sam. Underline each sentence in the passage that reflects an environmental or hereditary influence on Sam's health and well-being. Circle each sentence that reflects a behavior. Then rewrite the scene, changing Sam's behaviors in a way that will give the video—and his life—a chance for a happy ending.

It is 7 A.M. on a school day. The alarm clock next to Sam's bed sounds. Turning off the alarm, Sam struggles to a sitting position and yawns broadly. He is exhausted, having come home at 1:30 A.M. from an evening out with his friend Chris. Chris, who is two years older, is someone Sam looks up to, though Sam does wish Chris would stop ribbing him about his height. Like his father, Sam is just over 5 feet tall and is self-conscious about being short.

Sam's mother calls from the kitchen, telling him that breakfast is on the table. Sam ignores her as he slips into the soiled T-shirt and rumpled jeans he was wearing the night before. Entering the kitchen, Sam goes to the refrigerator and grabs a can of soda. His mother gently urges him instead to eat the homemade yogurt, fresh-baked bread, and sliced fruit she has set out for his breakfast. Without looking at his mother, Sam grumbles that he doesn't want breakfast.

A long blast from a car horn alerts Sam that his ride to school has arrived. Grabbing his knapsack, he heads out the door, nearly tripping on the toy his younger sister left on the front step. Sam angrily kicks the toy, then climbs into the passenger seat of his friend Mike's car. Ignoring the seat belt, Sam tosses his knapsack into the back seat as Mike floors the gas pedal and tears off down the street.

Your rewrite: _____

_____

_____

_____

_____

_____

_____

_____

_____

_____

_____

_____

_____

_____

ACTIVITY 3 **Applying Health Skills**

Charge!

Directions ➤ As noted in the lesson, a positive step toward wellness is accepting responsibility for your own health and for the health of others. Sometimes these two areas of responsibility overlap. An individual who drives safely, for example, demonstrates responsibility not only for his or her own health but for that of passengers in the same or other vehicles and even for pedestrians. The box below lists healthful behaviors. Rewrite each behavior in the appropriate area of the diagram below. Think carefully about all consequences for each behavior.

- Getting plenty of physical activity
- Staying in school to complete your education
- Preparing foods that are sources of good nutrition
- Being a positive role model
- Abstaining from the use of alcohol and other drugs

- Eating foods that are sources of good nutrition
- Getting plenty of rest each night
- Taking part in a neighborhood crime watch
- Helping a younger sibling with his or her homework
- Choosing not to litter
- Abstaining from sexual activity
- Finding a positive role model

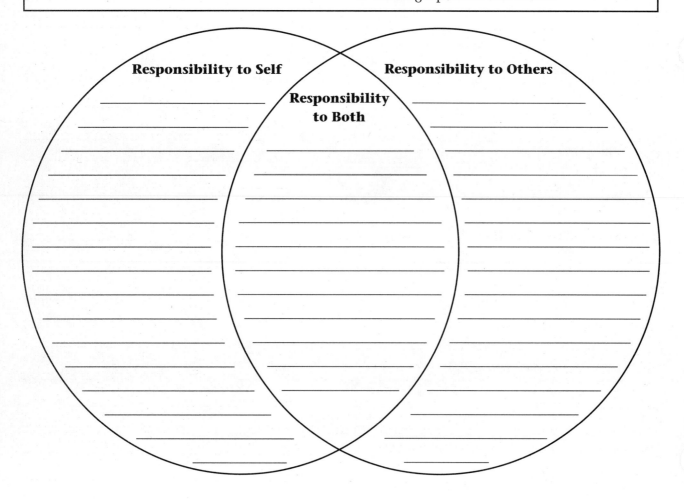

Responsibility to Self

Responsibility to Others

Responsibility to Both

CHAPTER 1 Study Guide

STUDY TIPS
- Read the Health Concepts for each lesson.
- Look up the meanings of any Health Terms that are unfamiliar.
- Read the questions below before you read the chapter.

Directions ➤ As you read the chapter, answer the following questions. Later you can use this guide to review the information in the chapter.

LESSON 1

1. Identify three characteristics of each of the following aspects of health.

   a) Physical health: _____

   _____

   _____

   _____

   _____

   b) Mental and emotional health: _____

   _____

   _____

   _____

   _____

   c) Social health: _____

   _____

   _____

2. Define *wellness*. _____

3. Identify four important lifestyle factors. _____

   _____

   _____

   _____

   _____

4. Define *health education* and describe its goal. _____

   _____

   _____

5. Identify two traits of a health-literate person. _____

   _____

LESSON 2

6. Give an example of how heredity influences a person's health.

_____

_____

7. Identify an aspect of a person's physical environment that can affect his or her health.

_____

_____

8. What are peers? Why are peers an important part of your social environment?

_____

_____

_____

9. Identify two aspects of your cultural environment.

_____

_____

10. How is behavior different from other influences on your health?

_____

_____

LESSON 3

11. Define risk factors.

_____

_____

12. Give an example of a cumulative risk.

_____

_____

13. What are two ways of demonstrating responsibility for the health of others?

_____

_____

14. Identify two main protective factors in a teen's life.

_____

_____

15. Define abstinence. How does abstinence contribute to one's health and behavior?

_____

_____

_____

CHAPTER 2 Vocabulary

health skills	self-esteem	goals
communication	stress	action plan
refusal skills		

Directions ➤ Words and phrases and the ideas they represent can be related in various ways.

■ Some terms can be described as a means to an end. Examples: *prevention → health; health education → health literacy.*

■ Some terms exist in a *cause-effect relationship*, in which a condition or event represented by one word is a possible cause of a condition or event represented by another. Examples: *fire → burn; thirst → drink.*

Use the information on word relationships to answer the questions that follow.

1. Explain how the term *action plan* is a means to an end.

_____

_____

_____

2. Write an original sentence that details what a breakdown in *communication* might cause. In your answer, try to use one or more terms from the above list.

_____

_____

_____

3. Discuss the cause-effect relationship between *self-esteem* and *refusal skills.*

_____

_____

_____

4. How does the term *health skills* represent both a means to an end and a cause of some condition or event?

_____

_____

_____

5. Name two terms from the above list that are related in some way to the term *goals.* Explain the relationship.

_____

_____

_____

ACTIVITY 4 Applying Health Skills

Guiding Light

Directions ➤ Ms. Rashid, the school's guidance counselor, is out sick today. You have been asked to fill in for her as a *peer counselor*—a student who assists other students in handling life problems. The following are brief descriptions of your caseload for today. Read each case description. Then decide what health skill or skills could most benefit each student.

1. Connie is currently dating Juno, a star running back on the varsity football team. She really likes Juno, but lately he has been pressuring her to become more intimate. Deep down, Connie feels she is not ready, but she is afraid of losing Juno.

   Recommended skill(s): _____

   _____

2. James is a failure. At least that is what other students at school keep telling him—and not just through their words. Just yesterday at lunchtime, James went to get a napkin, and when he returned to the table where he had left his lunch, it was gone. The grins on the faces of students nearby revealed they were involved. Rather than report the incident, James chose to go hungry.

   Recommended skill(s): _____

   _____

3. Paula is going through a difficult time at home. Her father was laid off from his job, and her parents have begun fighting a lot. All the tension is making it difficult for Paula to fall asleep at night, which has caused her schoolwork to suffer. She would like to tell her parents about her feelings, but she doesn't know how.

   Recommended skill(s): _____

   _____

4. Emma and Sally have been friends since second grade. Now they are not speaking. Last week Sally waited a half hour in front of the movie theater for Emma to show up. She later discovered that Emma had forgotten entirely about their date and had instead gone over to the house of another classmate. Emma has attempted to reach Sally by phone several times, but Sally isn't going to let her "ex-friend" off the hook that easily.

   Recommended skill(s): _____

   _____

ACTIVITY **5** **Applying Health Skills**

Noteworthy

I. Directions ➤ Alejandro is preparing a lesson on decision making to present to a middle school class. He has written his notes on index cards, which unfortunately have become scrambled. Help Alejandro out by putting his cards in order according to the six steps of the decision-making process. Write the appropriate number in the space before each index card.

Lucy tells Calvin that she has agreed to attend with someone else, but hopes he will call her again another time.

Lucy has long admired Calvin and would like to accept his invitation to the spring dance. Unfortunately, she has already agreed to go to the dance with Mitch.

Lucy has a wonderful time at the dance with Mitch and receives a phone call from Calvin a week later.

If Lucy breaks her date with Mitch, she risks hurting his feelings and leaving him without a date. If she refuses Calvin's invitation, she may never get another chance to go out with him.

Over the years, Lucy's family has instilled in her the importance of honoring commitments and making good on promises.

Lucy could simply break the date with Mitch, explaining that she had wanted to go with Calvin all along. Alternatively, Lucy could explain to Calvin that she already has a date but would very much like to go out with him some other time.

II. Directions ➤ Setting goals for yourself increases your chances for a healthful and successful life as an adult. Use the action plan form below to set a long-term goal. Consult the plan from time to time to chart your progress.

Personal Action Plan

1. The goal I will work on: _____

_____

2. Measures I will take to help me reach my goal: _____

_____

3. Sources of help and support: _____

_____

4. My time frame for reaching my goal: _____

_____

5. Checkpoints I will use to evaluate my progress: _____

_____

6. My reward to myself upon reaching my goal: _____

_____

CHAPTER 2 Study Guide

STUDY TIPS
- Read the Health Concepts for each lesson.
- Look up the meanings of any Health Terms that are unfamiliar.
- Read the questions below before you read the chapter.

Directions ➤ As you read the chapter, answer the following questions. Later you can use this guide to review the information in the chapter.

LESSON 1

1. Define *health skills.*

_____

_____

2. Name two social health skills.

_____

_____

3. Identify four steps involved in effective communication.

_____

_____

4. What are refusal skills?

_____

_____

5. Identify the five steps in the strategy of refusing.

_____

_____

6. What are two ways of building self-esteem?

_____

_____

7. What are three techniques for managing stress?

_____

_____

8. Name two strategies for accessing reliable information.

_____

_____

9. What are three things you should do when you need help with a problem?

_____

_____

LESSON 2

10. Which aspect of health literacy does the decision-making model support?

_____

11. State the six steps of the decision-making model. For each step except step 5, identify a question you should ask yourself.

Step 1: _____

_____

_____

Step 2: _____

_____

_____

Step 3: _____

_____

_____

Step 4: _____

_____

_____

Step 5: _____

_____

_____

Step 6: _____

_____

_____

12. What is a goal?

_____

_____

13. Give an example of both a long-term goal and a short-term goal.

_____

_____

14. Define *action plan*.

_____

_____

physical fitness	metabolism	cross-training
body composition	basal metabolism	overload
flexibility	calories	progression
muscular strength	aerobic exercise	specificity
muscular endurance	anaerobic exercise	warm-up
cardiorespiratory	isometric exercise	cool-down
endurance	isotonic exercise	resting heart rate
sedentary lifestyle	isokinetic exercise	

I. Directions ➤ In the box below are a number of word parts and their meanings. Use this information to answer the questions that follow.

aer- "atmospheric, gas"   *an-* "back, again"   *iso-* "same, equal"   *-metric* "related to measurement"

1. What word in the definition of *aerobic* is suggested by the presence of the prefix *aer-*? Explain your answer. _____

2. Which type of exercise might be defined literally as "using the same or equal measurement"? How does this literal definition relate to the one provided in the chapter? _____

   _____

3. Using the meaning of the prefix *an-* and the meaning of *aerobic*, what can you infer about the role of oxygen in anaerobic exercise? _____

   _____

II. Directions ➤ Fill in the terms from the list above with the corresponding definition.

_____ 4. The minimum amount of energy required to maintain the life processes in a body.

_____ 5. A gradual increase in overload necessary for achieving higher levels of fitness.

_____ 6. The ability to move a body part through a full range of motion.

ACTIVITY | **6** | **Applying Health Skills**

You Rate!

Directions ➤ The computer readouts below show the fitness scores of several students at Jefferson High School. Use the readouts along with the information from the lesson to rate each student's fitness levels for each test. Enter this information in the appropriate box in the "Rating" column. Then in the space provided at the bottom of each readout, offer specific fitness recommendations for each student.

1. Name	Gender	Age	Test	Score	Rating
Mohammed Nadim	Male	16	Flexibility	9 in.	
			Push-ups	16	
			Curl-ups	26	
			Leg Lifts	8	
			Step Test	124	

Recommendations:

2. Name	Gender	Age	Test	Score	Rating
Sylvie Switzer	Female	15	Flexibility	10 in.	
			Push-ups	4	
			Curl-ups	12	
			Leg Lifts	6	
			Step Test	127	

Recommendations:

3. Name	Gender	Age	Test	Score	Rating
Daniel Randazzo	Male	14	Flexibility	10 in.	
			Push-ups	15	
			Curl-ups	23	
			Leg Lifts	20	
			Step Test	104	

Recommendations:

ACTIVITY **7** Applying Health Skills

What the Doctor Ordered

Directions ➤ Dr. Caputo was called away on an emergency, but he has left behind his notes from intake sessions with four new patients. The notes appear in the numbered paragraphs below. Help the doctor out. In the spaces following each paragraph, write (a) the type of exercise program each patient ought to be advised to begin, and (b) any lifestyle changes the patient should be advised to make.

1. Patient, a 51-year-old male, works as a claims adjuster for an insurance company; spends most weekdays seated behind desk. Reports spending much of free time watching TV. When questioned, admitted he will drive one block to store to pick up a quart of milk rather than walk. Typical lunch during week includes visit to fast-food restaurant, located conveniently downstairs from office.

   Type of exercise: _____

   Lifestyle changes: _____

   _____

2. Patient is 28-year-old male construction worker. Has gained 27 pounds over normal weight in past six months, even though his labor is largely physical and involves considerable isokinetic activity. When questioned about eating pattern, reported taking part in numerous "tailgating" parties during football season, including excessive consumption of fried chicken wings and other foods high in saturated fat.

   Type of exercise: _____

   Lifestyle changes: _____

   _____

3. Patient is 32-year-old male recuperating after eight-month bout of chronic illness. Gets out of breath while walking. Has lost significant strength and muscle mass as a result of prolonged hospital stay. Currently 17 pounds under desirable weight for height and body frame.

   Type of exercise: _____

   _____

   Lifestyle changes: _____

   _____

4. Patient is 18-year-old student in pursuit of qualifying trials in Olympics-level gymnastics. Complains of being overweight, even though patient tests at 40th percentile of weight for age and body frame and states that he gives careful attention to what he eats. Pulse recovery rate, tested in office, reveals excellent results.

   Type of exercise: _____

   Lifestyle changes: _____

   _____

ACTIVITY   **8**   **Applying Health Skills**

My Personal Fitness Plan

Directions ➤   As noted in the lesson, realistic goals are essential to the success of an exercise program. Here is your chance to plan such a program for yourself and to reap the health dividends. Fill in Part I of the form below. Once you have begun your program, fill in Part II at the end of each week to help you monitor your progress.

PART I

Current lifestyle (for example, active, sedentary) _____

_____

Chief exercise goal (for example, to lose weight, to build endurance) _____

_____

Factors to consider in choosing an activity

1. Description of local geography: _____

2. My interests/strengths/weaknesses: _____

3. Health problems or conditions: _____

4. Time each day when I will exercise: _____

Other concerns or considerations _____

_____

PART II

	Number of sessions	Intensity (amount of weight/ achieved target heart range)	Duration (minutes, sets/reps)
End of Week 1			
End of Week 2			
End of Week 3			
End of Week 4			
End of Week 5			
End of Week 6			
End of Week 7			
End of Week 8			
End of Week 9			
End of Week 10			

CHAPTER **3** Study Guide

STUDY TIPS
- Read the Health Concepts for each lesson.
- Look up the meanings of any Health Terms that are unfamiliar.
- Read the questions below before you read the chapter.

Directions ➤ As you read the chapter, answer the following questions. Later you can use this guide to review the information in the chapter.

LESSON 1

1. Identify two benefits of physical fitness to each of the following areas of health.

    a) Physical health: _____

    _____

    _____

    _____

    b) Mental and emotional health: _____

    _____

    _____

    _____

    c) Social health: _____

    _____

    _____

    _____

2. Identify the five basic components of physical fitness, and define each.

    _____

    _____

    _____

    _____

    _____

    _____

    _____

3. Name the test used to measure upper body strength.

    _____

4. What aspect of fitness are leg lifts used to measure?

    _____

5. What is one way of measuring cardiorespiratory endurance?

    _____

LESSON 2

6. What three body systems directly benefit from regular exercise?

_____

7. What is metabolism? How is it affected by exercise?

_____

_____

8. Name two benefits of exercise to your emotional health.

_____

_____

_____

_____

9. What is aerobic exercise? What basic component of physical fitness does aerobic exercise improve?

_____

_____

_____

10. Name three types of anaerobic exercise.

_____

LESSON 3

11. Name four factors that need to be taken into account when selecting a program of physical activity.

_____

_____

12. Identify three principles of an effective workout.

_____

13. What are the three stages of an exercise session?

_____

14. What do each of the letters in *F.I.T.* stand for? Explain each of the terms.

_____

_____

15. Define *resting heart rate*. What is this number used for?

_____

_____

CHAPTER 4 **Vocabulary**

physical activity	power	sprain
lifestyle activities	training	overexertion
agility	hydration	heat cramps
balance	anabolic steroids	heat exhaustion
coordination	muscle cramp	frostbite
speed	strain	hypothermia
reaction time		

I. Directions ➤ Many of the terms listed above can be grouped with respect to a common idea or theme. The terms *agility* and *balance,* for example, can both be grouped under the general heading "Skills-Related Fitness Measures." Complete the chart that follows, adding a heading of your own to the column on the right. Extend the chart so as to use as many of the terms from the chapter as possible.

Skills-Related Fitness Measures	
agility	_____
balance	_____
_____	_____
_____	_____
_____	_____
_____	_____
_____	_____
_____	_____
_____	_____

II. Directions ➤ Complete the word web below with terms that reflect a cause-effect relationship with the relevant weather term.

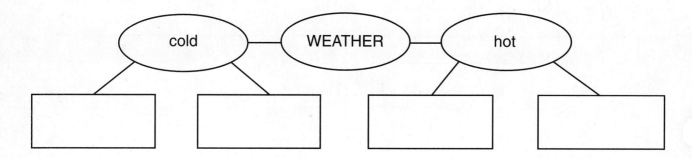

ACTIVITY 9 Applying Health Skills

Good Sports

Directions ➤ The Sports Connection is a consulting and training service that helps individuals choose a physical activity that is right for them. The following are profiles of two of the Connection's clients. Read each profile, including the remarks about the client's personal likes and dislikes. Rate each client's performance in each area of fitness, writing your rating in the blank sections of the profile. Then recommend a sport or other activity for each client, explaining your recommendations.

1.

Gender	Area of Sports-Related Fitness	Score	Rating
Male	Agility	30	
	Balance	3	
	Coordination	9	
	Speed	70 yd.	
	Reaction Time	19 in.	
	Power	15	

Client's Remarks: I am looking for a sport or activity I can do with my friend.

Recommendations: _____

_____

_____

2.

Gender	Area of Sports-Related Fitness	Score	Rating
Female	Agility	17	
	Balance	6	
	Coordination	7	
	Speed	64 yd.	
	Reaction Time	20 in.	
	Power	21	

Client's Remarks: I would like to spend more time with my family—by which I do *not* mean sitting in front of the TV in our den. I am not sure what kind of activity I would like for us all to get involved in. I *can* tell you that the one time we went camping in the wilderness, my teenage sons loved the experience.

Recommendations: _____

_____

_____

_____

ACTIVITY 10 Applying Health Skills

Out With the Old

Directions ➤ As in other areas of health and wellness, ideas about physical fitness have changed over time. Notions that were once regarded as current have been replaced by more up-to-date, scientific ones. The passage below contains views about fitness that were common at the turn of the twentieth century. Draw a line through each view that runs counter to the ideas and recommendations presented in the lesson. Then, in the space corresponding to the sentence number for that view, write the current recommendation.

Health To-Day   *39*

Aspects of Physical Fitness

(1) When selecting a pastime that will assist the reader in the pursuit of improved physical health, it is well not to overlook activities that may be done as part of one's daily routine (so-called leisure activities). (2) One must be firm in selecting one—and only one—such activity; pursuit of several simultaneous activities has been shown to be counterproductive to the goal of improved health. (3) Several additional caveats [warnings] must be adhered to; viz:

☞ (4) Suspend consumption of all food and/or beverage both prior to and during vigorous activity; experience has revealed that such consumption tends to cause gastric disease and detracts from the benefits of the activity.

☞ (5) Endeavor to get sufficient sleep after and preceding vigorous physical activity, inasmuch as bed rest renews and re-invigorates the body. (6) Some complain of difficulty falling asleep; to those I would advise performing their chosen physical activity within the hour prior to retiring and by so doing deplete the body's energy and induce slumber.

(7) Some of my patients have inquired as to whether it is wise to take part in team activities or athletic contests such as the game called town-ball [an early version of baseball] or turning [an ancient sport]. (8) In response to such query, I offer an emphatic "No"; team and partner activities breed competition, an evil of modern living.

(1) _____

(2) _____

_____

(3) _____

(4) _____

_____

(5) _____

(6) _____

(7) _____

(8) _____

ACTIVITY 11   **Applying Health Skills**   FOR USE WITH
CHAPTER 4, LESSON 3

At the Club

Directions ➤   You have been hired by a health club as a troubleshooter and adviser. Your job is to counsel members on sensible rules of exercise and to take action when injuries and other health-related emergencies arise. On the lines below each description, write the action you would take and the advice you would give. Use information in the lesson to help you determine the appropriate response.

1. On some days, Rose Kingston attends the club's aerobics class, while on others she rides the stationary bicycle. Today Rose decides to do both activities. She is on the bicycle for ten minutes when suddenly the muscle in her left leg contracts tightly and will not relax.

   Action you take: _____

   _____

   Advice for the future: _____

   _____

2. It is a hot, humid day. Shiro Hoshikawa, a new client, has been doing laps on the outdoor track for the past hour. All of a sudden, another member rushes up to you and reports that a club member out on the track appears dizzy and nauseated and cannot seem to catch his breath. Upon reaching the track, you find that Shiro's skin is pale and moist.

   Action you take: _____

   _____

   Advice for the future: _____

   _____

3. Ben Epstein, who is overweight, joined the club to shed some pounds. Although the temperature outside today is 93 degrees and the humidity level is high, Ben is determined to make up for lost time by playing tennis with a fellow member. Halfway through the first set, Ben collapses. You rush over to administer first aid and discover that his pulse is racing and his skin is dry and hot to the touch.

   Action you take: _____

   _____

   Advice for the future: _____

   _____

CHAPTER 4 Study Guide

STUDY TIPS
- Read the Health Concepts for each lesson.
- Look up the meanings of any Health Terms that are unfamiliar.
- Read the questions below before you read the chapter.

Directions ➤ As you read the chapter, answer the following questions. Later you can use this guide to review the information in the chapter.

LESSON 1

1. Briefly explain each of the following types of physical activity.

   a) Lifestyle activity: _____

   _____

   b) Sports activity: _____

   _____

2. Name and define the six measures of skills-related fitness.

   _____

   _____

   _____

   _____

   _____

   _____

3. Name the test used to measure agility. _____

4. What aspect of fitness is the stick toss and catch used to measure? _____

5. Explain how reaction time is measured. _____

LESSON 2

6. What is training, and why is training necessary for playing sports?

   _____

   _____

7. Name three components of a good training program.

   _____

8. What is hydration? _____

9. Name six negative consequences of taking anabolic steroids.

   _____

   _____

   _____

10. In what ways can competition be a positive force?

_____

_____

_____

LESSON 3

11. Name and describe three common minor exercise-related injuries to the muscular and skeletal systems.

_____

_____

12. Give the four steps of the R.I.C.E. procedure for treating minor strains and sprains.

a) R. _____

b) I. _____

c) C. _____

d) E. _____

13. Name and describe four major exercise-related injuries that require medical attention.

_____

_____

_____

_____

14. Define and tell how each of the following weather-related health risks can be avoided.

a) Overexertion: _____

_____

b) Heat cramps: _____

_____

c) Heat exhaustion: _____

_____

d) Frostbite: _____

_____

e) Hypothermia: _____

_____

15. Name four things you can do to minimize the risk of injury when playing sports.

_____

_____

CHAPTER 5 Vocabulary

nutrients	proteins	Recommended Dietary
hunger	amino acids	Allowances (RDA)
appetite	lipid	food additives
nutrition	linoleic acid	enriched food
carbohydrates	cholesterol	fortification
glucose	vitamins	unit pricing
glycogen	minerals	

I. Directions ➤ Complete the passage below by writing the correct term from the list in each blank.

Many people's eating habits are governed by _____—a psychological desire—rather
(1)
than _____—actual need. People should eat foods that contain the
(2)
_____ and _____ that help regulate vital body processes.
(3)   (4)

The body converts the _____ in foods such as pasta and bread to
(5)
_____ , a simple sugar that is the body's chief fuel. It is stored in the liver and muscles
(6)
as _____ . The body uses _____—which contains chemical
(7)   (8)
substances called _____ —to help build and maintain body tissue. One thing the
(9)
body does *not* need from food is _____ , a fatlike substance in foods of animal origin.
(10)

Some processed foods contain _____ , put in them for various purposes.
(11)
Manufacturers produce _____ by adding back nutrients lost in processing or use
(12)
_____ by which nutrients not naturally present are added to food.
(13)

II. Directions ➤ Two of the words in the list above, *nutrients* and *nutrition*, contain the same root,
nutri-. This root comes from the Latin word *nutrire*, meaning "to nourish." List
below as many other words as you can that are derived from *nutrire*. Then write a
brief paragraph using at least three of those words.

_____

_____

_____

_____

_____

_____

_____

ACTIVITY 12 Applying Health Skills

Overheard

Directions ➤ The following are fragments of overheard conversations or messages. Read each fragment. Then, on the lines provided, identify the factor that has influenced the speaker's food choices or that is being used to influence the listener's food choices.

1. *[Spoken into telephone.]* Hi, honey, it's Liz. I'm going to have to work late tonight. After you pick up Ruthie at ballet class, would you mind stopping off and ordering a pizza to bring home? Thanks a bunch. I promise, I'll cook tomorrow!

   Factor: _____

2. *[To friend.]* Well, yes, I did just finish dinner. I suppose I could just tag along with you guys to the restaurant and . . . you know, maybe order a dessert or something.

   Factor: _____

3. *[Voice of announcer overheard on TV.]* And remember, every Tuesday at Mario's is Sicilian Night. Fourteen authentic mouth-watering Old World recipes to choose from, all just like Mama used to make!

   Factor: _____

4. *[Woman to friend over lunch.]* I swear, Elise, I'm so mad at Arthur—I can't begin to tell you. Why, the other night, I baked and ate an entire pan of brownies. I was so upset!

   Factor: _____

5. *[Male teen sitting behind wheel of car to friend in passenger seat.]* Wanna grab a bite? I just heard about this new joint over on Security Boulevard. All you can eat for five bucks—good deal, huh?

   Factor: _____

6. *[Two elderly women on park bench.]* That's right, Sarah. We're going to my son and daughter-in-law's home again for Thanksgiving. I don't honestly know what to tell you. Last year, they served some kind of—what do you call it, tofu?—thing. Who ever heard of Thanksgiving without turkey?! I have a good mind to stay home, and cook dinner myself. . . .

   Factor: _____

ACTIVITY 13 Applying Health Skills

Pro-TEEN

I. Directions ➤ To meet the demands of a more active lifestyle and the growth spurt associated with the teen years, your body needs more protein now than it may later in life. How much protein do you specifically need? To find out, multiply your body weight by the appropriate number in the chart below. The result will be your recommended daily allowance of protein expressed in grams. Enter your personal information on the lines that follow.

If you are between . . .	. . . and . . .	. . . multiply by
the ages of 11 and 14	do light activity	0.45
the ages of 15 and 18	do light activity	0.40
the ages of 11 and 18	are very active	0.55

My age: _____

Type of activity I routinely do: _____

Amount of protein I should eat: _____

II. Directions ➤ Jamie has decided to become a vegetarian. She is willing to eat dairy products but no animal products. Below are some foods that can be found in the refrigerator and pantry at Jamie's house. From these possible ingredients, assemble three lunch menus that would give Jamie the complete proteins she needs as a growing teen.

Refrigerator	**Pantry**
• Quart of milk	• Package of freeze-dried tomato soup
• Cold chicken	• Saltine crackers
• Block of sharp cheddar cheese	• Jar of grape jelly
• Container of cooked black beans	• Uncooked pasta
• Broccoli	• Loaf of whole-grain bread
• Package of baked ham	• Bag of raw peanuts
• Container of strawberry yogurt	• Bottle of ketchup
	• Taco shells

Lunch menu 1: _____

Lunch menu 2: _____

Lunch menu 3: _____

ACTIVITY 14 Applying Health Skills

Vitamania

Directions ➤ Although eating sensibly provides your body with all the vitamins and minerals it needs, many Americans attempt to satisfy their daily requirement for these essential nutrients through pills and other supplements. Apart from concerns health experts have raised about the effectiveness of vitamin and mineral supplements, an even larger issue for many consumers is manufacturers' credibility. When buying vitamin and mineral supplements, the consumer must have a firm grasp of the facts. Such knowledge is the only protection against false claims and boasts. Below is a page from a web site advertising supplements. Read the claims. Then explain any misinformation in the chart that follows.

| _ | 🗗 | X |

| Back | Forward | Home | | Reload | Images | | Stop |

Location: http://www.caveat-emptorium.com/health.htm/#vita-sist

Vita-sist Tablets   Order #459772; bottle of 100; $49.95 plus $3 s. & h.
Don't like spinach or broccoli? No problem. Get a bountiful helping of much-needed vitamin K with Vita-sist tablets, a miraculous blend of the body's essential water-soluble vitamins, including K, A, and folic acid. Vitamin K is important for tissue growth and tooth development. Vita-sist tablets also promote healing and aid your body in its manufacture of B complex vitamins. Because the nutrients in Vita-sist pass harmlessly from the body through liquid wastes, the tablets are guaranteed safe. Will make you feel like a new person after just a week!

Fountain of Youth Mineral Water   Order #310254; 32 oz. $17.95 plus $4 s. & h.
Perfect for the athlete in training. FOY helps rid your body of harmful electrolytes, while providing ample supplies of sodium and potassium. Best of all, FOY provides selenium, a vitamin essential to healthy teeth, which is not found in any food! Get your whole family started on FOY. You'll be glad you did.

Vita-sist Tablets	Fountain of Youth Mineral Water
_____	_____
_____	_____
_____	_____
_____	_____
_____	_____
_____	_____
_____	_____
_____	_____
_____	_____
_____	_____
_____	_____
_____	_____

ACTIVITY 15 **Applying Health Skills**

What's for Dinner

Directions ➤ For most Americans, dinner is the big meal of the day. More important, it is an opportunity to make up for essential servings of foods from the various food groups that you may have missed earlier in the day. Below are Health Journal entries of two teens reflecting what they have eaten so far today. Plan a dinner menu for each that will help them satisfy their minimum nutritional needs for the day. Include any general recommendations you may have about each teen's eating patterns.

Tanya's Health Journal

My food selections for 9/10.

Breakfast:

- whole-grain muffin
- cup of yogurt

Lunch:

- 2-ounce chicken breast over pasta
- string beans
- fresh apple
- carton of milk

Afterschool snack:

- wedge of melon
- package of snack crackers

Dinner:

- _____

_____

_____

_____

_____

_____

Recommendations: _____

_____

_____

_____

_____

Will's Health Journal

Today is Sept. 10. So far I have eaten:

For breakfast—

- jelly doughnut
- glass of milk
- glass of orange juice

For lunch—

- peanut butter and jelly sandwich
- can of soda

Snack—

- eight cookies
- glass of milk

Dinner—

- _____

_____

_____

_____

_____

_____

Recommendations— _____

_____

_____

_____

_____

9. Tell how minerals differ from vitamins.

_____

LESSON 4

10. Define Recommended Dietary Allowances (RDA).

_____

11. Tell why each of the following guidelines is important to good health.

a) Eat a variety of foods.

_____

b) Balance the foods you eat with physical activity.

_____

c) Choose plenty of grain products, vegetables, and fruits.

_____

12. Tell why it is important to eat the following only in moderation.

a) Fats: _____

_____

b) Sugars: _____

_____

c) Salt and sodium: _____

_____

LESSON 5

13. Name three kinds of information that the government requires on food labels.

_____

_____

_____

14. List three reasons that food additives are added to foods.

_____

_____

15. Define unit pricing.

_____

_____

_____

CHAPTER 6 Vocabulary

overweight	anorexia nervosa	foodborne illness
obesity	bulimia nervosa	contaminant
underweight	electrolytes	pasteurized
undernutrition	rehydration	perishable
body mass index	carbohydrate loading	cross-contamination
(BMI)	vegans	food allergy
nutrient-dense	nutrient supplements	food intolerance
weight cycling	megadoses	

I. Directions ➤ Many of the terms listed above can be grouped with respect to a common idea or theme. The terms *overweight* and *underweight*, for example, can both be grouped under the general heading "Eating Problems." Complete the chart that follows, adding a heading of your own to the column on the right. Extend the chart so as to use as many of the terms from the chapter as possible.

Eating Problems	_____
overweight	_____
underweight	_____
_____	_____
_____	_____
_____	_____
_____	_____

II. Directions ➤ The term *pasteurized* from the list above is made up of two word parts—the root *pasteur,* from the name of the nineteenth-century bacteriologist Louis Pasteur, and the suffix *-ize,* meaning "become." Together the parts name the process Pasteur discovered for slowing the growth of pathogens in food.

1. The root *hom-* means "one and the same." Find a term in the dictionary relating to another food process that means "become one and the same." _____

2. The word part *hydr-* means "water." What term in the list has as part of its meaning the idea of "water again"? _____

3. What other word in the list has *hydr-* as one of its parts? What is the literal meaning of that term?

_____

_____

4. The word *contagious* means "capable of infecting by contact." What terms in the list with a structure similar to *contagious* also have to do with the spreading of infection?

_____

5. Judging from the definition of the term *megadoses,* what do you suppose the word part *mega-* means? Confirm your hunch using a good dictionary. _____

Name _____ Date _____ Class Period _____

ACTIVITY 17 Applying Health Skills

FOR USE WITH
CHAPTER 6, LESSON 1

You've Got a Case

Directions ➤ A doctor who specializes in weight management has more patients than she can handle. You have been asked to assist by reviewing the case studies of people who suffer from various weight-related problems. Review each case. Then, in the space provided, identify the problem each person faces. Finally, offer recommendations for overcoming that problem.

1. Lila's approach to losing excess weight is very simple. She simply does not eat for a couple of days at a time.

   Problem: _____

   _____

   Recommendations: _____

   _____

2. Willy has been underweight since he was a small child. Now that he is in his teens, he is self-conscious about his "stringbean" appearance. Worse still, the school doctor has advised him that being underweight carries nearly as many health risks as being overweight. Willy is trying to gain some pounds by eating high-fat snacks each day after school. He has also sworn off all physical activity for the time being for fear of burning off even more calories.

   Problem: _____

   _____

   Recommendations: _____

   _____

3. Ayda is always on or off a weight-loss program. For every 20 pounds she loses, she usually winds up gaining back 25.

   Problem: _____

   _____

   Recommendations: _____

   _____

4. Up until last month, Arturo was delighted with the slow but steady progress he was making at losing weight. Then suddenly and for no apparent reason, the pounds stopped coming off. Arturo is so discouraged he feels like drowning his sorrows in a large bowl of rocky road ice cream.

   Problem: _____

   Recommendations: _____

   _____

Copyright © Glencoe/McGraw-Hill

GLENCOE HEALTH • STUDENT WORKBOOK **33**

ACTIVITY 18 Applying Health Skills

A Losing Proposition

Directions ➤ The lesson mentions a number of fad diets and risky weight-loss strategies. Below are some others that have been investigated and in some cases banned by the U.S. Food and Drug Administration (FDA). Read the descriptions of these diet gadgets. Then use the information to answer the questions that follow.

- **Diet patches.** Worn on the skin much in the manner of nicotine patches, these devices have been proved ineffective and unsafe. The FDA has seized millions of these products from manufacturers and promoters.

- **Starch blockers.** Falsely claiming to interfere with the body's digestion of starches, these pills have "rewarded" their users instead with nausea, vomiting, diarrhea, and stomach pains.

- **Electrical muscle stimulators.** These devices, which have a legitimate use in physical therapy treatment, are promoted as being able to induce weight loss while toning the body. When used without professional supervision, however, the stimulators can cause electrical shocks and burns.

- **Appetite-suppressing eyeglasses.** Nothing more than ordinary eyeglasses with colored lenses, this gadget supposedly projects an image to the back of the eye that dampens the desire to eat. There is no evidence that these glasses work. A related gadget, "magic weight-loss earrings," has likewise been exposed as a fake.

1. Which of the devices described above sounds the silliest to you? Explain your reaction.

   _____

   _____

   _____

2. What general trends or patterns can you find among the various gadgets?

   _____

   _____

   _____

3. Americans spend an estimated $30 billion a year on diet programs and products. Why do you suppose the public is willing to spend its hard-earned cash on gadgets like these?

   _____

   _____

   _____

4. Based on the information about the products above, what questions do you think health consumers should ask before investing in a weight-loss product or plan?

   _____

   _____

   _____

ACTIVITY 19 Applying Health Skills

Weekly Mailbag

Directions ➤ You are the author of a weekly advice column in a teen magazine. Below are three of the letters you received this week. Answer each using information from the lesson.

1. Dear Mailbag:

I am on my school's track team. Today after practice some of the guys on the team got into this big debate on what you should eat before a meet. Franky, who's pretty sharp academically, says he knows for a fact that the thing to eat is steak—and lots of it. Gil saw this show on the Sports Network that said the thing to load up on is spaghetti. I want to do my part to help us place in the regionals next week. Who should I believe?

Mike L., age 16

Dear Mike:

_____

_____

_____

Good luck in the regionals, Mailbag

2. Dear Mailbag:

I am dating this really cute guy. We get along well and like being together. The only problem we have is finding a place to eat. I love double cheeseburgers, and he doesn't eat any meat or chicken or anything like that. In fact, he's always trying to get me to stop eating meat, too. I think I read someplace that avoiding meat altogether isn't that good for you.

Jenetta S., age 17

Dear Jenetta:

_____

_____

_____

Happy eating, Mailbag

3. Dear Mailbag:

Tryouts for football start next week. I know I could make the team if only I weighed 10 pounds more. I've been doing everything for the past couple weeks to put on pounds, but nothing is working.

Shawn J., age 16

Dear Shawn:

_____

_____

_____

See you at game time, Mailbag

ACTIVITY 20 Applying Health Skills

Cooking with Carla

Directions ➤ Carla has a cooking show on TV that is taped before a live audience. Recently, eight audience members became ill within several hours of sampling one of the creations Carla cooked during a broadcast. Read the transcript of the show, and underline any sentence or phrase that may account for the outbreaks of foodborne illness. Then in the spaces provided, tell what steps Carla can take in the future to avoid the same unhappy result.

Carla: Now that we have cut up our chicken, we will begin cooking the pieces. *[Sets down knife. Begins transferring chicken pieces from cutting board to pot.]* Be careful not to drop the pieces into the hot oil, since it may splash up and burn you. Instead, set the pieces gently into the pot. *[Finishes transferring chicken pieces.]* There. Now let's turn our attention to the vegetables that will go in the pot with the chicken. *[Picks up onion from countertop and places on same cutting board as before break.]* You want to chop your onion finely. *[Picks up knife and begins to cut onion.]* Notice I am using the same knife I used to cut up the chicken. This particular knife has a good sharp blade, which makes the job of chopping much quicker. It also reduces the risk of cutting yourself. *[Picks up cutting board and, using back of knife, slides chopped onion into pot.]* Now we cover the dish and let it cook for a full five minutes. Remember, you never want to eat poultry that is not cooked through. Okay, let's pretend that five minutes have passed and we have allowed the dish to cool to room temperature. Over here, I have a version of the dish that I prepared earlier. It has had nearly two and a half hours to cool. Look how lovely this chicken looks. *[Tilts pot toward camera.]* You can see how the poultry has retained a little of its pink color. If you like your chicken a little less rare, you can always cook it another minute or so.

Steps Carla can take in the future:

_____

_____

_____

_____

_____

_____

_____

_____

_____

_____

_____

CHAPTER 6 Study Guide

STUDY TIPS
- Read the Health Concepts for each lesson.
- Look up the meanings of any Health Terms that are unfamiliar.
- Read the questions below before you read the chapter.

Directions ➤ As you read the chapter, answer the following questions. Later you can use this guide to review the information in the chapter.

LESSON 1

1. What are calories?

_____

2. Explain the difference between overweight and obesity.

_____

_____

3. Tell why each of the following conditions is a hazard to health.

a) Obesity: _____

_____

_____

b) Underweight: _____

_____

_____

_____

4. What is body mass index, and why is it used?

_____

_____

LESSON 2

5. Define *weight cycling*.

_____

6. Name two other risky weight-loss strategies.

_____

7. Give two reasons why teens sometimes develop eating disorders.

_____

8. Explain the differences between anorexia nervosa and bulimia nervosa.

_____

_____

_____

LESSON 3

9. Define *electrolytes*, and explain what an athlete can do to maintain electrolyte balance.

_____

_____

10. Define *carbohydrate loading*, and explain why some athletes follow this practice.

_____

_____

11. Explain the difference between a vegetarian diet and a vegan diet.

_____

_____

12. Name two groups of people that can benefit from taking nutritional supplements.

_____

LESSON 4

13. Define *pasteurized*.

_____

_____

14. Give one way to minimize risks of foodborne illness during each of the following stages of food buying and preparation. Any one of each of the following:

a) Buying: _____

_____

b) Pre-preparation: _____

_____

_____

c) Cooking: _____

d) Handling leftovers: _____

_____

15. Explain the difference between a food allergy and a food intolerance.

_____

_____

_____

_____

CHAPTER **7** **Vocabulary**

sweat glands	plaque	retina
acne	periodontal disease	external auditory
sebaceous glands	tartar	canal
follicles	lacrimal gland	ossicles
dandruff	sclera	labyrinth
periodontium	cornea	otosclerosis
pulp	choroid	tinnitus

Directions ➤ Complete the word map by writing each related word under its correct heading.

Structures of the Skin

_____

_____

_____

Structures of the Ear

_____

_____

_____

Problems of the Skin

_____

_____

Problems of the Ear

_____

_____

PERSONAL HEALTH

Structures of the Teeth and Gums

_____

_____

Structures of the Eye

_____

_____

_____

_____

Problems of the Skin

_____

_____

_____

ACTIVITY **21** Applying Health Skills

The Play's the Thing

Directions ➤   Read the one-act play below. Then answer the questions that follow.

[Lydia, Jeanette, and Manny—three teen friends—have driven to the beach for the day. They are wearing bathing suits and are seated on beach towels.]

Lydia: *[Looking glumly up at sky, then at wristwatch, which reads 4:30.]* I can't believe this. We've been here for six hours, and most of that time it's been overcast!

Manny: Relax. We have the whole summer to work on our tans.

Jeanette: Who feels like going for a dip?

Lydia: Not me! If the sun does peek through, I don't want to miss the rays. *[Picks up plastic bottle labeled "baby oil." Spreads liberally over arms and legs.]*

Manny: *[Looks over at Jeanette.]* I'll join you for a dip. *[His eyes suddenly focus on her shoulder.]* Hold on, you've got a fly on you.

Jeanette: I hope it's not one of those green beach flies! Those things sting! *[Gingerly, Manny reaches over and swats at Jeanette's shoulder. She winces in pain.]* Ouch!

Manny: Did I miss the fly and hit you?

Jeanette: *[Looking back over shoulder with concern.]* No, I think I'm getting a burn.

Lydia: *[Voice showing disbelief.]* How can you get a burn? There's no sun out!

1.   At what hour did the teens arrive at the beach? What health risk is associated with the hours during which they were exposed to the sun's UV rays?

_____

_____

2.   In one of Manny's speeches, he notes a "goal" the three teens are working on for the summer. What is the goal, and why is it unhealthful?

_____

_____

3.   What misconception about sun safety can be found in Lydia's second speech?

_____

_____

4.   What long-term risks does the future hold in store for the teens?

_____

_____

5.   What advice would you give these teens?

_____

_____

ACTIVITY 22   **Applying Health Skills**

Dear Diary

Directions ➤ The passages that follow are entries from the diaries of two different individuals. The entries provide a "window" on the personal dental hygiene of their authors. For each entry, identify the health problem or problems the person may be facing. Then write what changes in behavior he or she can make to reduce the risks.

1. Hi, Diary:

   Chess club ran late. Running short on cash, so grabbed a candy bar for lunch, then rushed to study hall to get ready for my history exam. Met Lynn and Bruce at the soda shop after school and caught up on old times. Also finally had a chance to sample that new flavor of ice cream I've been meaning to try—triple chocolate chunk; it's great! Studied after dinner, then watched a little TV. Feeling too tired once again to wash up, brush, etc., so just turned in around 9:00.

   Potential problem(s): _____

   _____

   _____

   Changes that will reduce risks: _____

   _____

   _____

2. Dear Diary:

   Did my laundry and grocery shopping after work. Went out of my way to pick up a bottle of that mouthwash Connie told me about. (Have that big date with the cute guy from accounting next week!) Hope the mouthwash is everything Connie says. With the way my breath has been smelling lately, I really need something strong.

   Potential problem(s): _____

   _____

   _____

   Changes that will reduce risks: _____

   _____

   _____

| ACTIVITY **23** | **Applying Health Skills** | FOR USE WITH
CHAPTER 7, LESSON 3 |

Dictionary Definition

Directions ➤ Below is part of a page from a dictionary. Each head word (the word in boldface) has to do with some aspect of eye problems and/or their treatment. Use the dictionary entries and information from the lesson to answer the questions that follow.

ophthalmologist *n.* [more at OPHTHALMOLOGY] medical doctor with specialty in ophthalmology, capable of measuring problems of the eye and treating eye infections and other disorders.

ophthalmology *n.* [Gk *optos,* "eye," + *ology,* "study"] 1. branch of medicine concerned with the study of the eyes, their physiology and structure, and the diseases and conditions affecting them. 2. field of inquiry concerned with refraction, orthoptics (the treatment of defective visual habits), the prevention of blindness, and the care of the blind.

optician *n.* craftsperson who makes corrective lenses.

optometrist *n.* [more at OPTOMETRY] 1. doctor of optometry. 2. practitioner who has passed state licensing examination after graduation from a 4-year school that offers degree in doctor of optometry (O.D. or D.O.S.).

optometry *n.* [Gk *optos,* "eye," + Gk *metrein,* "to measure"] 1. profession concerned with vision problems. 2. measurement of eyes (by an optometrist [*see*]) and prescription of corrective lenses.

O
P

1. Which professional would you consult if you were experiencing symptoms of nearsightedness? Explain your response.

   _____

   _____

   _____

2. If you were told by an eye care professional that you needed eyeglasses, would you then set up an appointment with an ophthalmologist? Why or why not?

   _____

   _____

   _____

3. An older relative is experiencing blurry and hazy vision and complains of having difficulty seeing at night. Would you recommend that the person see an optometrist? Why or why not?

   _____

   _____

   _____

ACTIVITY 24 **Applying Health Skills**

Hear, Hear

Directions ➤ The distance at which a sound can be heard depends on its intensity. This property is measured in units called *decibels* (dB). The bar graph below shows a spectrum, or range, of intensities experienced by the human ear. The thresholds at the lowest and highest ends represent, respectively, the point at which a human is able to detect any sound at all and the point at which a sound is so intense as to cause serious physical damage to the ear. Use the graph to answer the questions that follow.

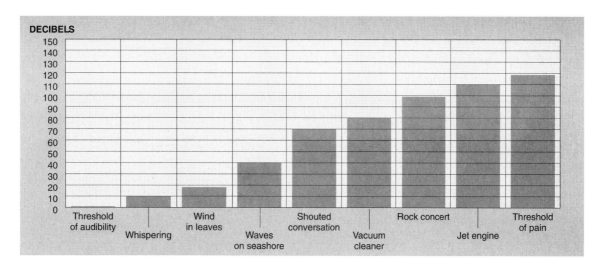

1. The sound of a rush-hour traffic jam is approximately 91 dB. If you were going to create a bar for this item on the graph, between which two items would it fall?

    _____

2. Based on the graph, what would you estimate the intensity of each of the following to be? Explain your response.

    (a) The sound of gentle rain falling on pavement: _____

    Explanation: _____

    (b) The crowd noise in the final moments of a varsity football game in which the score is tied:

    _____

    Explanation: _____

3. How close would the intensity of the sounds at a rock concert be to the threshold of pain? Explain your response.

    _____

    _____

4. Based on your answer to the previous question, what precautions should teens take when attending rock concerts and similar events?

    _____

    _____

| CHAPTER | **7** | **Study Guide** |

STUDY TIPS
- Read the Health Concepts for each lesson.
- Look up the meanings of any Health Terms that are unfamiliar.
- Read the questions below before you read the chapter.

Directions ➤ As you read the chapter, answer the following questions. Later you can use this guide to review the information in the chapter.

LESSON 1

1. Describe the function of sweat glands.

_____

2. Define *sebaceous glands*.

_____

3. Identify three steps you can take to have healthy skin.

_____

_____

_____

4. Give one way to control each of the following hair problems.

a) Dandruff: _____

_____

b) Head lice: _____

_____

LESSON 2

5. Define *peridontium*.

_____

6. What is the difference between plaque and tartar?

_____

_____

_____

7. Briefly explain each of the following problems.

a) Halitosis: _____

b) Gingivitis: _____

c) Periodontitis: _____

d) Malocclusion: _____

LESSON 3

8. Give a definition for each part of the eye listed below.

a) Sclera: _____

b) Cornea: _____

c) Choroid: _____

d) Retina: _____

9. What is the difference between nearsightedness and farsightedness?

_____

_____

_____

10. Explain two ways in which amblyopia may be treated.

_____

_____

11. Which disease of the eye is characterized by clouding of the lens, which causes blurring or hazy vision and problems with night vision?

_____

LESSON 4

12. What is the function of the fine hairs and tiny wax-producing glands of the external auditory canal?

_____

13. What are the ossicles, and where are they located?

_____

14. Name two things you can do to keep your ears healthy.

_____

_____

_____

15. Describe each type of hearing loss listed below.

a) Conductive deafness: _____

_____

_____

b) Sensorineural deafness: _____

_____

_____

CHAPTER **8** Vocabulary

mental health	personality	phobias
feedback	psychologist	hostility
hierarchy of needs	modeling	defense mechanisms
aesthetic	emotions	resilience
self-actualization	empathy	

Directions ➤ An analogy compares two words or ideas in a way that shows some similarity or relationship between them. An *analogy sentence* is an analogy in which one of the terms is missing and must be inferred. For example, in the analogy sentence *numbers is to mathematics as _____ is to language*, the missing term, words, might be arrived at using the following logic: "In just the way numbers are the basic units of mathematics, so words are the basic units of language." Complete each analogy sentence below by writing one of the words or phrases from the above list.

1. physician is to body as _____ is to mind

2. feelings are to emotions as irrational fears are to _____

3. feedback is to _____ as health education is to physical health

4. _____ is to identification as insensitivity is to disinterest

5. aesthetic is to _____ as vegetable group is to Food Guide Pyramid

6. spiders are to phobias as denial is to _____

7. caring is to friend as _____ is to enemy

8. attitudes are to _____ as skeleton is to body

9. pity is to compassion as buoyancy is to _____

10. _____ is to satisfaction as self-centeredness is to rejection

11. behavior is to _____ as actions are to imitating

12. hunger is to physical as beauty is to _____

CHAPTER 8 Study Guide

STUDY TIPS
- Read the Health Concepts for each lesson.
- Look up the meanings of any Health Terms that are unfai   r.
- Read the questions below before you read the chapter.

Directions ➤ As you read the chapter, answer the following questions. Later you   use this guide to review the information in the chapter.

LESSON 1

1. Define *mental health*.

_____

_____

2. Describe two roadblocks to mental health.

_____

_____

3. Explain the difference between feedback and self-talk.

_____

_____

LESSON 2

4. Who developed the hierarchy of needs presented in this chapter?

_____

5. Name the four basic categories of needs in order from most basic to most fulfilling.

_____

_____

6. Name two emotional needs according to the hierarchy of needs.

_____

7. What is the term for a complex set of characteristics that makes you unique and sets you apart from everyone else?

_____

8. Define *modeling*.

_____

_____

LESSON 3

9. What is the term for the ability to imagine and understand how someone else feels?

_____

10. Define *phobias*.

_____

11. Explain how anger differs from hostility.

_____

_____

LESSON 4

12. What are defense mechanisms? Name three defense mechanisms.

_____

_____

13. Give two constructive ways in which a person can express anger.

_____

_____

_____

14. Explain how a person can deal healthfully with guilt.

_____

_____

_____

15. Define *resilience*.

_____

_____

CHAPTER 9 Vocabulary

stress	stress tolerance	support ___ ___p
eustress	Type A personality	time mana___ ___ent
stressor	Type B personality	skills
distress	hardy personality	priorities
alarm	psychosomatic	grief reaction
adrenaline	response	delayed grief
resistance	rechanneling	response
fatigue	relaxation response	closure

Directions ➤ Read the following passage. For each underlined phrase, write the term from the list above that can replace it.

The response to (1) <u>the body's and mind's reactions to everyday demands or threats</u> is different for each individual and may vary depending on the (2) <u>stimulus that produces this response.</u> (3) <u>Negative stress</u> can result when there is too much pressure or trauma and you do not know how to cope with it. (4) <u>Positive stress</u>, on the other hand, can help you achieve your goals.

About one in ten Americans have a low (5) <u>ability to handle stress</u>. Some people may even develop a (6) <u>physical disorder that results from stress</u>. This is related to personality. Some people have a (7) <u>personality type that seems to stay healthy regardless of the degree of stress</u>. A (8) <u>competitive, high-achieving personality type</u> is most likely to develop heart disease from stress. The (9) <u>laid-back, noncompetitive personality type</u> is less likely to suffer from stress.

There are three stages of stress. During (10) <u>the first stage, when the body and mind go on high alert</u>, the adrenal glands produce (11) <u>a hormone to prepare the body to respond</u>. If the condition lasts, (12) <u>the stage when the body tries to repair its damage and return to normal</u> occurs. The last stage is (13) <u>a tired feeling that lowers one's level of activity</u>.

1. _____

2. _____

3. _____

4. _____

5. _____

6. _____

7. _____

8. _____

9. _____

10. _____

11. _____

12. _____

13. _____

ACTIVITY 29 **Applying Health Skills**

Frame-up

Directions ➤ In addition to stress management skills, tools exist for confronting stressors head-on before stress has a chance to build. One of these is a process called *reframing*. Reframing is seeing a negative situation in a new, more positive light. For example, instead of viewing a person as stingy, you might tell yourself that he or she is thrifty. Each passage below contains a negative statement, followed by a partial reframing of the situation. Complete each reframing in the space provided.

1. The test is going to cover ten chapters? Preparing for it is going to be a real nightmare. I might as well just give up now and admit I'm licked.

   Reframed situation: The test is going to cover ten chapters? Preparing for it is a going to be a real

   _____

   _____

   _____

2. The thing I hate most about Paul is that he is bossy. He's always taking charge and telling everyone else what to do.

   Reframed situation: The thing I admire most about Paul is

   _____

   _____

   _____

3. Margaret's biggest weakness is that she is so picky. She always analyzes everything from every angle.

   Reframed situation: Margaret's biggest strength is

   _____

   _____

   _____

ACTIVITY 30 **Applying Health Skills**

On the Job

Directions ➤ As personnel director for a big-city newspaper, you are interviewing applicants for the job of metro editor. The individual who lands the position will be in charge of a staff of 40 employees and will be responsible for getting out two editions of the paper every day. In addition, the hours are long, and the deadlines are tight. Below are profiles of the three most promising applicants to date. Review the applications. Then answer the questions that follow.

Applicant 1: Graduated in upper third of class at large college. Ten years of newspaper experience, two as assistant editor, remainder as reporter. Took year off to travel, see world. Pastimes include painting and nature walks. Smiled much of the time during interview. Appeared laid-back, at ease.

Applicant 2: Seventeen years of experience as features editor for daily newspaper in Chicago. Graduated third in class from large university; served on honors society. Published two books. Drummed fingers throughout interview; kept rearranging self in chair. Pastimes include tennis, though suffers from bronchial asthma, forcing occasional periods of inactivity.

Applicant 3: After stint in Vietnam as chopper pilot, attended small university; graduated tenth in class. Four years of newspaper experience, assisting metro editor on small-town newspaper. Devotes time to volunteer work. Family history of high blood pressure. Very attentive and pleasant during interview. No problem relocating across the country if awarded position.

1. Match each of the applicants to one of the personality types shown. Explain how you arrived at your answer in each case.

   Type A personality: _____

   _____

   Type B personality: _____

   _____

   Hardy personality: _____

   _____

2. Which applicants suffer from medical conditions that could be affected by stress? Identify those conditions.

   _____

3. Identify pros and cons for each applicant regarding the person's suitability for the position. Use the back of this page if you need more space.

   Applicant 1: _____

   _____

   Applicant 2: _____

   _____

   Applicant 3: _____

   _____

ACTIVITY 31 **Applying Health Skills**

Slice of Life

Directions ➤ As noted in the lesson, time management skills can help you control the stress in your life. Complete the time management profile below. Then answer the questions that follow.

Time Management Profile

■ Activities I typically do in a 24-hour period during the school week (for example, homework, afterschool activities, phone conversations with friends, band practice, TV, video games, computer, eating, sleeping):

_____

_____

■ Time spent doing each of the above activities:

Activity 1: _____   Activity 5: _____

Activity 2: _____   Activity 6: _____

Activity 3: _____   Activity 7: _____

Activity 4: _____   Activity 8: _____

■ Activities I typically do in a 24-hour period during the weekend:

_____

_____

■ Time spent doing each of the above activities:

Activity 1: _____   Activity 5: _____

Activity 2: _____   Activity 6: _____

Activity 3: _____   Activity 7: _____

Activity 4: _____   Activity 8: _____

■ On a separate piece of paper, make two pie graphs to represent the amount of time you devote to various activities. Make one graph for weekdays, the other for weekends.

---

1. Which details of your time management profile, if any, did you find surprising? Explain.

_____

2. Did your blend of activities show a balance of time for family friends, work, and fun?

_____

3. Are there more healthful and efficient ways you could slice up your time "pies"? In other words, would dividing up the time differently reduce stresses in your life? Explain.

_____

ACTIVITY 32 **Applying Health Skills**

At a Loss

Directions ➤ The following are descriptions of losses various people have suffered. Read each description. Then identify each person's stage in the grief process.

1. A week has passed since Marcella noticed during gym class that the locket she had been wearing around her neck was gone. The locket had been passed down through several generations of Marcella's family. She still can't believe that it's gone.

   Stage: _____

2. The reality has finally settled in for Tram that her cat Tippy, who was run over and killed a month ago, is gone from her life. Tram has begun to go out again with her friends and even managed to smile yesterday after recalling some of the funny things Tippy used to do.

   Stage: _____

3. Umberto has been feeling awful ever since he failed to make tryouts for the school baseball team. He spends much of his time alone in his room with his thoughts.

   Stage: _____

4. Now that Connie has broken off their relationship, Ed keeps staring at her picture. He has even begun speaking to it, begging Connie's image to take him back.

   Stage: _____

5. Chip's bike was stolen five days ago. "I'd just love to get my hands on the creep who took it," Chip told his brother after school today. Then Chip pounded his fist into his other hand.

   Stage: _____

CHAPTER 9 **Study Guide**

STUDY TIPS
- Read the Health Concepts for each lesson.
- Look up the meanings of any Health Terms that are unfamiliar.
- Read the questions below before you read the chapter.

Directions ➤ As you read the chapter, answer the following questions. Later you can use this guide to review the information in the chapter.

LESSON 1

1. What is the difference between distress and eustress?

_____

2. Name three of the five categories of stressors.

_____

_____

3. What two body systems are active during the stress response?

_____

4. Tell what changes take place in the body and/or mind during each of the three stages in the stress response.

a) Alarm: _____

_____

b) Resistance: _____

_____

c) Fatigue: _____

_____

5. Name three different kinds of fatigue.

_____

LESSON 2

6. How does a Type A personality differ from a Type B personality?

_____

_____

_____

7. Name three characteristics of the hardy personality.

_____

ACTIVITY 33 **Applying Health Skills**

Help!

Directions ➤ On the lines below each situation presented, write what you think the person's problem might be and what he or she should do.

"I really don't know what is the matter with my cousin. One moment he seems to feel good and makes all these plans with me to do things. Then, all of a sudden, he says he just doesn't feel like doing anything. Sometimes I can't get a word in edgewise because he won't stop talking. At other times trying to get one word out of him is like pulling teeth. What do you think is wrong?"

Possible problem: _____

Course of action: _____

_____

_____

_____

"I was sexually assaulted about a year ago, and it took me quite a while to get over it. Last week I was waiting for a train at a station I had never been to before. Something about the station—the noises there, the people—brought the whole experience back to me, even though the attack didn't take place in a train station. Why is this affecting me so much now? I thought I had put this all behind me."

Possible problem: _____

Course of action: _____

_____

_____

_____

"My husband is convinced someone is after him. When I question him about it, he gets this funny look on his face—as though he is no longer sure he can even trust me. He is behaving very strangely. He quit his job. He has stopped showering, shaving, and even changing his clothes."

Possible problem: _____

Course of action: _____

_____

_____

_____

ACTIVITY **34** Applying Health Skills

The Changing Face of Mental Health ....

Directions ➤ Today suicide is not only viewed as a serious health problem but is considered an unlawful act in the United States and many other countries. This was not always the case. Read the passage below. Then answer the questions that follow.

Suicide—the intentional taking of one's own life—is a distinctly human act that has appeared in all societies from earliest times. In ancient Rome, suicide was widely regarded as an act of honor. A similar view was held a continent away in Japan. The Japanese custom of *hara-kiri* dictated that an individual who had failed atone by ritual impalement on a richly ornamented dagger. Hara-kiri as a voluntary form of execution was abolished in 1868.

During the Middle Ages, the act of suicide was seen throughout Europe as both a sin and a crime. In England, the land and goods of anyone committing suicide automatically became the property of the state. This law remained on the books through the mid-1800s. The family of a suicide victim, however, could always get around it by getting the medical examiner to declare that the person had been insane.

Ritual suicide enjoyed a brief comeback in Japan during World War II. Japanese *kamikaze* pilots considered it an honor to perform suicidal missions by crashing their airplanes into an enemy target.

1. In what way was the attitude toward suicide during the Middle Ages different from the one held in earlier times? In what ways was suicide less understood than it is today?

    _____

    _____

    _____

    _____

2. The ancient Romans believed in the philosophical doctrine of Stoicism, which underscored the importance of disregarding pain. In what ways does this explain their attitude toward suicide?

    _____

    _____

    _____

3. What aspect of the conditions during the Second World War may have constituted a risk factor for pilots who volunteered for *kamikaze* missions?

    _____

    _____

    _____

    _____

ACTIVITY 35 **Applying Health Skills**

Doctor in the House

Directions ➤ The patient profiles below come from the files of a large mental health clinic. The clinic has a variety of health professionals on staff. From each profile, determine the type of professional treating the patient. State the reasons for your assumption.

Patient 1: Patient currently under care of Dr. Stephan. Receiving individual counseling twice a week and group therapy twice a week. Progress has been made in dealing with anxiety reaction.

Type of health professional: _____

Reasons for assumption: _____

_____

_____

Patient 2: Dr. Mesa's patient. Suffers from extreme and sometimes violent mood swings. Has been placed for time being on mild dose (viz. 50 mg b.i.d.) of chlorpromazine. Suitability of other antipsychotic medications currently under evaluation.

Type of health professional: _____

Reasons for assumption: _____

_____

_____

Patient 3: Case has been referred to Dr. Yapolitano due to suspicion of organic foundations; psychoneurosis. Prior care included anxiolytic-sedative medications (e.g., diazepam) prescribed by Dr. Mesa.

Type of health professional: _____

Reasons for assumption: _____

_____

_____

Patient 4: Under care of Mr. Rash. Patient, who is depressive, has benefited from one-on-one sessions.

Type of health professional: _____

Reasons for assumption: _____

_____

_____

CHAPTER 10 Study Guide

STUDY TIPS
- Read the Health Concepts for each lesson.
- Look up the meanings of any Health Terms that are unfamiliar.
- Read the questions below before you read the chapter.

Directions ➤ As you read the chapter, answer the following questions. Later you can use this guide to review the information in the chapter.

LESSON 1

1. Briefly describe each of the following anxiety disorders.

   a) Phobia: _____

   _____

   b) Obsessive-compulsive disorder: _____

   c) Panic disorder: _____

   d) Post-traumatic stress disorder: _____

   _____

2. Which mental disorder describes an illness in which a person complains of disease symptoms, but no physical cause can be found?

   _____

3. Which group of mental disorders involves mood swings or mood extremes which interfere with everyday living?

   _____

4. Name and describe two kinds of personality disorders.

   _____

   _____

   _____

   _____

5. Which mental disorder means "split mind"?

   _____

LESSON 2

6. What is the term that means feelings of helplessness, hopelessness, and sadness?

   _____

7. Name two risk factors for suicide.

   _____

   _____

8. List three nonverbal or behavioral suicide warning signs.

_____

_____

_____

_____

_____

_____

_____

9. Name three things you can do if you suspect someone you care about is considering suicide.

_____

_____

_____

_____

10. What are cluster suicides?

_____

_____

LESSON 3

11. Which type of medical doctor specializes in diagnosing and treating mental disorders?

_____

12. Briefly explain the treatment for each type of mental disorder.

a) Psychotherapy: _____

_____

b) Medical psychotherapy: _____

_____

c) Psychoanalysis: _____

_____

13. Which type of medical doctor specializes in organic disorders of the brain and nervous system?

_____

14. What can a psychiatrist do that a clinical psychologist cannot do?

_____

15. What does a psychiatric social worker do?

_____

_____

CHAPTER 11 Vocabulary

relationship	compromise	active listening
friendship	empathy	body language
role	communication	constructive criticism
cooperation	"I" message	

Directions ➤ A number of different relationships exist among words and phrases and the ideas they represent.

- A *hierarchical relationship* is a relationship in which one word is higher in rank than another. Examples: *president — vice president; employer — employee.*
- A *cause-effect relationship* is a relationship in which a condition or event represented by one word is a possible cause of a condition or event represented by another. Examples: *fatigue — sleep; hunger — eat.*
- A *parallel relationship* is a relationship in which two or more words share an equivalent status. Examples: *mother — father; conversation — discussion.*

Use the information on word relationships to answer the questions that follow.

1. In what way might the terms *active listening* and *constructive criticism* be said to exhibit a parallel relationship?

_____

_____

2. Write an original sentence that shows a hierarchical relationship between the terms *relationship* and *friendship.*

_____

_____

3. Explain the effect that cooperation and compromise can have on a relationship.

_____

_____

4. *Speaking* and *listening* are two terms from the chapter that have a hierarchical relationship with one of the terms in the list above. Identify that term. Name two phrases from the list that have the same relationship with that term.

_____

_____

_____

5. Explain the cause-effect relationship between the terms *empathy* and *friendship.*

_____

_____

ACTIVITY 36 Applying Health Skills

On a Role

Directions ➤ Below are fragments of two conversations that Terrence Daily, a teen, had this past week. Read each passage. Then answer the questions that follow.

[Monday, 5:23 P.M.]

Terrence *[To woman watering lawn next door.]:* Good evening, Ms. Lake.

Ms. Lake *[Smiling.]:* Oh, hello, Terrence. Aren't you getting home late from school today, dear?

Terrence: No, ma'am, I had band practice after school. *[Remembering something.]* By the way, Ms. Lake, I found this on the sidewalk on my way to school this morning. *[Removing change purse from backpack and handing it to woman.]* I think it's yours.

Ms. Lake: Oh, thank you, Terrence! It's such a relief to have this back. Here, let me give you something for your trouble. *[Reaches inside change purse.]*

Terrence: No trouble at all, Ms. Lake! I know how worried you must have been.

[Wednesday, 6:19 P.M.]

Terrence *[Rising from table.]:* That was a great dinner, Mom.

Mrs. Daily *[Noticing Terrence heading out of kitchen.]:* Not so fast, young man. You have a sink full of dinner dishes to do.

Terrence *[Looking surprised.]:* It's Wednesday. It's Kiva's night to clean up after dinner. *[Looks in direction of 10-year-old girl, who sits finishing her dinner.]* Besides, I've got plans.

Mrs. Daily: I'm afraid you'll have to break them, honey. I guess I forgot to tell you: Kiva has to go over to her school tonight. She volunteered to help out with the book sale to raise funds for the new library. Do the dishes for her tonight, and tomorrow she'll do your chores.

Terrence: Well—I guess that's fair. First, let me call my friend Jess and let him know I can't make it tonight.

1. Name two of Terrence's roles. _____

2. Name two of Terrence's relationships. _____

3. What trait of a healthy relationship does Terrence exhibit in his willingness to do Kiva's chore?

_____

4. Explain how each of the following traits of a healthy relationship is revealed through Terrence's words and actions: Possible answers:

Loyalty: _____

Empathy: _____

_____

Trustworthiness: _____

Respect: _____

Dependability: _____

ACTIVITY 37 **Applying Health Skills**

Letter Perfect

Directions ➤ Below are fragments of personal letters. Read each fragment. Then identify the letter as either a criticism or an acknowledgment, tell whether it is positive or negative in tone, and if negative, explain how the letter writer could better communicate the same ideas.

1.

> To whom—or what—it may concern:
> My new "clock radio" (if that is what you can call it!) arrived in pieces. I don't guess it would ever occur to you to pack the junk you sell so that it doesn't break. I will be contacting my lawyer . . .

Criticism or acknowledgment: _____

Positive or negative: _____

Better way to communicate: _____

_____

2.

> Dear Mr. Flatley,
> As president of the Jefferson High debating society, I want to congratulate you as faculty adviser and the Milford team on their fine showing in the regional finals. While my teammates and I are disappointed at having been eliminated, we feel that in losing to Milford, we have lost to worthy opponents and, in so doing, feel no disgrace . . .

Criticism or acknowledgment: _____

Positive or negative: _____

Better way to communicate: _____

_____

3.

> Dear Jan,
> I felt under the circumstances that writing was easier than phoning. We have been friends for a long time, so I am trying hard to understand how this mess got started. The only conclusion I can come to is that it is all your fault! How could you have done such a hurtful, spineless, backbiting, mean-spirited thing to someone you call a friend? . . .

Criticism or acknowledgment: _____

Positive or negative: _____

Better way to communicate: _____

_____

CHAPTER **12** Vocabulary

sibling	child abuse	crisis center
affirmation	emotional abuse	foster care
custody	neglect	family counseling
domestic violence	exploitation	mediator
spousal abuse		

Directions ➤ Etymology, the study of a word's origins, can provide clues to the meanings of an entire family of words and phrases. Using a dictionary that contains the etymology of words, investigate the origins of each word and phrase listed above. Then answer the questions that follow.

1. Which term in the list comes from an Old English word meaning "food" or "feeding"?

   _____

2. One of the terms in the list can be traced at least in part to a Middle French word meaning "home." Which term is this? Identify and define at least four other dictionary entries that have the same etymology.

   Term from list: _____

   Other terms and their meanings: _____

   _____

   _____

3. Which term has the same root as the word critical ("relating to a turning point or juncture")? From what Greek word do both terms arise? What is its meaning?

   _____

4. Which term descends from a Latin root meaning "be in the middle"? Name two other dictionary entries that share that root.

   Term from list: _____

   Terms that share root: _____

5. One term in the list shares a common root with the dictionary entry *confirm*. Identify the term and its etymology. Explain why its origin is appropriate to its current meaning in English.

   _____

   _____

   _____

ACTIVITY **38**	**Applying Health Skills**	FOR USE WITH CHAPTER 12, LESSON 1

Lost and Profound

Directions ➤ The items below were turned in at the lost and found department of a local mall. Examine each item. Then answer the questions that follow.

A. Personal diary; inside cover contains inscription reading, "Property of Juanilla Jones, 123 W. 7th Street, Midland City". Most recent entry notes, "Today I got a 93 on my month-long history project. I guess hard work really does pay off."

B. Shopping list with the following handwritten notes:

"—Stop in at Martinson's to see if Grandma's heirloom clock will be repaired in time for family gathering at Thanksgiving.

—Go to bakery and buy cake to celebrate Junior's winning tristate swimming competition."

C. Receipt from a department store with the following items: "One pair of shoes (boys' dept.); one ski parka (boys' dept.); one sweater (junior misses)."

D. Gold religious pendant on chain; inscription on back reads, "To Maria, with love, Mom and Dad."

1. Which of the items at the lost and found reflect an emphasis on family culture and/or traditions? Explain.

_____

_____

_____

_____

2. Which of the items suggest a family in which emotional needs of the children are met? Which suggest a family in which basic needs are met? Explain.

_____

_____

_____

_____

3. Which of the items suggest a family in which values are instilled in the children? Explain.

_____

_____

_____

_____

ACTIVITY 39   **Applying Health Skills**

Nightmares on Elm Street

Directions ➤   Elm Street is like any other average residential street in any American city. Through a remarkable coincidence, however, Elm Street in the past several months has experienced a disproportionately high number of family problems. A number of them are described below. Read each description, and identify the problem—or problems.

1. Lucinda, age five, lives at Number 304 with her mother and sister Chloë, age two. Lucinda hasn't seen her father in ten months. Lucinda's mother is so distraught that she ignores Lucinda and Chloë for days at a time.

   Problem(s): _____

   _____

   _____

2. The family at Number 366 have just brought a new baby home from the hospital—their seventh. The other children in the household, ranging in age from 4 to 11, are resentful. Neither parent has worked in close to four months, and the older children are aware that there is barely enough money to feed those already living in the house.

   Problem(s): _____

   _____

   _____

3. Neighbors have become suspicious of activities at Number 347. The one adult female in the house frequently emerges wearing sunglasses, and even the thick coating of makeup she applies fails to cover the bruises.

   Problem(s): _____

   _____

   _____

4. When the Jamiesons moved into Number 300 last month, Mr. Jamieson had to be helped up the stairs by a nurse. The Jamieson children appear well-behaved and seem to be weathering their parents' divorce.

   Problem(s): _____

   _____

   _____

ACTIVITY 40 **Applying Health Skills**

Help Is on the Way

Directions ➤ Below are descriptions from a directory of community social services. Read each description. Then identify the type of help (for example, support group, mediation) each service provides.

1. Life Line, 672 Ward Street, 555-7127. Regular weekly sessions and meetings for families and family members experiencing a wide range of problems, from abuse to neglect. Reasonable fees. A chance to grow by listening to and sharing stories with other people who have problems similar to yours.

_____

2. Raymond Bennett, Ph.D., 582 Foley Street, 555-6873. Clinical Psychology. Specialty: therapy for families and couples. Adjustable fee scale.

_____

3. Memorial Clinic, 7985 Gilchrest Boulevard, 555-1165. Our fully trained staff of over 40 licensed medical, mental health, and social service professionals are here to provide families in distress with all essential services, from counseling to shelter and hot meals. Battered women and men welcome. We are a state-run facility.

_____

4. Susan Robinson, M.S.W., 147 Red Street, 555-8356. If you are a couple experiencing marital difficulties, I can help. I have served the community for over seven years, listening to problems and helping couples reconcile their differences. Ask about our sliding scale of fees.

_____

5. The Greater South City Foundling Hospital, 3039 Park Avenue, 555-9047. For over 50 years, GSCFH has been placing unwanted and neglected children with loving, nurturing families.

_____

CHAPTER **13** Vocabulary

platonic friendship	infatuation	pa~~s~~~~ive~~
clique	peer pressure	agg~~re~~sive
prejudice	manipulation	asse~~rtiv~~e
stereotype	refusal skills	

Directions ➤ An analogy compares two words or ideas in a way that shows so___ ___ilarity or relationship between them. An *analogy sentence* is an analogy in w___ ___e of the terms is missing and must be inferred. For example, in the analogy ___e *hawk is to bird as* _____ *is to dog*, the missing term, *beagle*, might be arriv___ ___g the following logic: "In just the way a hawk is a type of bird, so a beagl___ ___e of dog." Complete each analogy sentence below by writing one of t___ ___ or phrases from the above list.

1. weak is to strong as _____ is to aggressive

2. racism is to _____ as sadness is to depression

3. timid is to insecure as _____ is to confident

4. thought is to idea as group is to _____

5. _____ is to unique as negative is to positive

6. hostility is to extreme dislike as _____ is to exaggerated love

7. pushy is to _____ as sad is to unhappy

8. _____ is to underhandedness as cooperation is to openness

ACTIVITY 41 **Applying Health Skills**

Waverley Hills 50505

Directions ➤ Below is a description of the relationships among the characters in a television pilot for a new soap opera. The new show involves teens at a typical high school. Read the description. Then answer the questions that follow.

CARLOS, the show's star, has many friends and acquaintances, among them RORY—his next-door neighbor—and BERNARD, with whom he shares a locker at school. CARLOS spends much of his time, however, with MAE and PHIL, who have been his best buddies ever since he moved to Waverley Hills six months earlier. The three are able to share their deepest feelings, and in the first episode, MAE is expressing the pain she feels over her recent breakup with ERNIE. As the three sit talking at a cafeteria table, TROY, MELISSA, and their group enter. TROY informs the three in his typically superior way that the table they are sitting at is *his group's* and that "not just anyone" can sit at that table.

1. Identify two characters who share a platonic relationship. Explain what makes the relationship platonic.

   _____

   _____

2. Identify two characters who share a casual friendship.

   _____

   _____

3. Identify the type of relationship Mae had with Ernie.

   _____

   _____

4. What aspects of Carlos's relationship with Phil and Mae identifies it as a close friendship?

   _____

   _____

5. What are groups like Troy and Melissa's called? What is the danger of such groups?

   _____

   _____

   _____

ACTIVITY 42 **Applying Health Skills**

FOR USE WITH
CHAPTER 13, LESSON 2

No Way!

Directions ➤ As noted in the lesson, people experiencing negative peer pressure can respond in three ways—passive, aggressive, and assertive. Read each situation below. Then identify the way in which the teen has responded to the pressure. If the response was *passive* or *aggressive*, suggest an assertive response.

1. A group of teens were watching TV at Cal's house when an ad for beer came on. Several people began to boast about drinking. When Ari remained silent, he was promptly challenged to drink one of the beers in Cal's family's refrigerator—or admit he was a wimp. Ari knew that Cal's parents were due home any minute, but he also knew that he would never live down the taunting if he refused. "Well, maybe . . . ," he said, his voice trailing off.

Ari's way of responding: _____

Assertive response: _____

_____

_____

2. Alfonso, who is 5 feet, 6 inches tall, just made the basketball team. When one of the older members of the team offered him pills that would have him "slam-dunking the ball in no time flat," Alfonso replied, "Thanks, but no thanks. The coach wouldn't have chosen me unless he thought I had something to offer. I'll take my chances being short."

Alfonso's way of responding: _____

Assertive response: _____

_____

_____

3. Ted sat behind Howie in history. Tomorrow the class would be taking an exam that counted for a third of their grade. Ted begged Howie to let him copy off Howie's paper. "It's easy," Ted assured him. "Just move your hand each time you write an answer. Come on, I'll give you 20 bucks if you do it." Howie looked Ted directly in the eye. "All I have to do is tell the assistant principal about our little conversation, and you'll get booted out of school so fast your head will spin. Now *bug off!*"

Howie's way of responding: _____

Assertive response: _____

_____

_____

4. Kim is tired of her 19-year-old neighbor's "coming on" to her all the time. Yesterday, when he suggested they take a ride in his new car, she replied, "Get lost!"

Kim's way of responding: _____

Assertive response: _____

_____

_____

CHAPTER 13 Study Guide

STUDY TIPS
- Read the Health Concepts for each lesson.
- Look up the meanings of any Health Terms that are unfamiliar.
- Read the questions below before you read the chapter.

Directions ➤ As you read the chapter, answer the following questions. Later you can use this guide to review the information in the chapter.

LESSON 1

1. What is the difference between a casual friendship and a close friendship?

_____

_____

_____

_____

2. Define *platonic friendship*.

_____

_____

3. What is a clique?

_____

_____

4. Give two ways in which being a part of a clique may be damaging.

_____

_____

5. Explain the difference between prejudice and a stereotype.

_____

_____

_____

_____

6. Define *infatuation*.

_____

_____

LESSON 2

7. What is peer pressure?

_____

_____

8. Give an example of positive peer pressure.

_____

_____

_____

9. Give an example of negative peer pressure.

_____

_____

_____

10. Define *manipulation.*

_____

_____

11. List three means of manipulation.

_____

_____

12. Explain the passive way of responding to negative peer influence.

_____

_____

13. Explain the aggressive way of responding to negative peer influence.

_____

_____

14. Explain the assertive way of responding to negative peer influence.

_____

_____

15. Give the three-step process for using assertive refusal skills.

   a) Step 1: _____

   b) Step 2: _____

   c) Step 3: _____

CHAPTER 14 Vocabulary

conflict	mediation	random violence
interpersonal conflict	peer mediators	aggravated assault
internal conflict	confidentiality	carjackings
escalate	violence	abuse
conflict resolution	homicide	sexual assault
tolerance	assailant	rape
negotiation		

Directions ➤ Use the clues to solve the puzzle. Write one letter of each answer in the space provided. The circled letters will spell out a key concept in resolving conflicts and preventing violence.

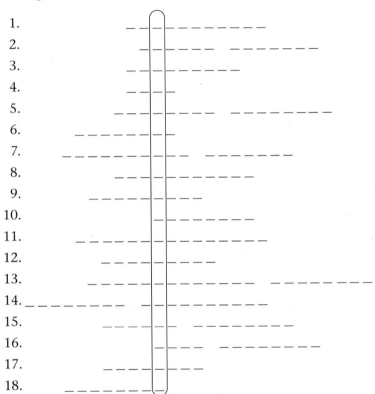

1. _ _ | _ _ _ _ _ _ _
2. _ _ | _ _ _ _ _ _ _ _
3. _ _ | _ _ _ _ _ _
4. _ _ |
5. _ _ | _ _ _ _ _ _ _ _ _
6. _ _ _ _ | _ _
7. _ _ _ _ _ _ | _ _ _ _ _ _
8. _ _ _ | _ _ _ _
9. _ _ _ _ | _ _
10. _ _ | _ _ _
11. _ _ _ _ _ | _ _ _ _ _
12. _ _ _ _ | _ _
13. _ _ _ _ _ | _ _ _ _ _ _ _ _
14. _ _ _ _ _ _ _ | _ _ _ _ _ _
15. _ _ _ | _ _ _ _ _ _
16. | _ _ _ _ _ _ _ _
17. _ _ _ | _ _
18. _ _ _ _ _ |

1. Stealing cars by force
2. An intentional sexual attack
3. Person who commits a violent act
4. Sexual intercourse by force
5. Struggles within yourself
6. Use of physical force
7. Unlawful attack with intent to hurt or kill
8. Ending a conflict by cooperating and problem solving
9. Conflict resolution with the aid of specially trained people

10. Murder
11. Respecting others' privacy and keeping details secret
12. Accepting others' differences
13. Disagreements between groups
14. Using compromise to reach agreement
15. Violence for no particular reason
16. Student trained to help other students
17. Any disagreement, struggle, or fight
18. Grow into an unhealthful situation

Key Concept: _____

ACTIVITY 43 **Applying Health Skills**

Party of the First Part

Directions ➤ As noted in the lesson, conflicts are a normal part of life. They arise whenever the wants, needs, wishes, demands, values, or beliefs of one person clash with those of another. Below is a story involving typical teens. Read the story. Then answer the questions that follow.

When Merrilee entered the kitchen, her older sister Corinna was on the phone. "Great, Lonny," Corinna was saying to her boyfriend. "See you at eight."

"Lonny's coming over?" Merrilee asked warily, as Corinna replaced the telephone receiver.

"Lonny and a few other friends are coming over," Corinna responded.

An alarm went off in Merrilee's head. "You're not having a party tonight, are you?" she asked, remembering her parents' orders before leaving for the weekend.

"Yes, I'm having a party," Corinna replied pointedly. "What's it to you, anyway?"

"It's just that Mom and Dad were very specific about—"

"Mom and Dad are forever babying both of us," Corinna said, interrupting. "You're just too blind to see that. How I'd love to go on chatting with you, Sis," she added sarcastically, "but I've got some planning to do." She then left the kitchen.

Merrilee wrestled with herself over whether to report Corinna's disobedience to her parents when they got back. Corinna was always at odds with their parents, and if Merrilee told them what happened, Corinna would be in deep trouble. If she didn't tell, she would be betraying her parents' trust.

1. Which of the teens is experiencing an internal conflict? What is the nature of this conflict?

_____

_____

_____

2. Name two parties in the story who experience ongoing interpersonal conflict with Corinna.

_____

_____

3. Identify a remark or action by Corinna that might escalate the conflict growing between her and Merrilee.

_____

_____

4. Which conflict revolves around values? What value is at the core of the conflict?

_____

_____

ACTIVITY 44 **Applying Health Skills**

Combating Schisms and Isms

Directions ➤ A *schism* (pronounced SIZ-uhm) is a split within a group. An example of a schism is students in a school forming factions to fight along racial lines. *Ism* is a suffix that means "belief system." Many words ending in *-ism* relate to prejudice. Examples of negative *isms* are *racism* (prejudice against members of an ethnic group), *sexism* (prejudice against members of a gender group—usually the one opposite the speaker's own), and *ageism* (prejudice against people of different age groups, often senior citizens). For each term below, identify an example and a conflict resolution skill that might prove useful.

1. **Ism:** Ageism.

   Example: _____

   _____

   Conflict resolution skill: _____

   _____

   _____

2. **Ism:** Racism.

   Example: _____

   _____

   Conflict resolution skill: _____

   _____

   _____

3. **Ism:** Sexism.

   Example: _____

   _____

   Conflict resolution skill: _____

   _____

   _____

ACTIVITY 45 **Applying Health Skills**

Calling All Cars

Directions ➤ Below are calls that have come in over the police radio on a given night. Identify the factor or factors involved in each act of violence. Then state actions you as an individual can take to avoid becoming involved in such incidents.

1. "All units in the vicinity of Fifth and Main head to 17364 Main. Holdup in progress. Assailants are armed and dangerous."

    Factors: _____

    Actions: _____

    _____

2. "Officer reported 'down' at Charleston and Elm following high-speed pursuit of carjacked vehicle. Perpetrator fired off three rounds before escaping scene on foot."

    Factors: _____

    Actions: _____

    _____

3. "Backup units needed at Thomson Park. Brawl between two downtown gangs over turf. Half a dozen injured."

    Factors: _____

    Actions: _____

    _____

4. "Vehicles near intersection of 18th and Forrestal, please respond. Suspected drive-by shooting. Two victims, one DOA at County General."

    Factors: _____

    Actions: _____

    _____

5. "Units head to Chanin Building. Possible 'leaper' on ledge, 31st floor. Appears intoxicated. Quoting lines from film in which celebrity threatened to end life."

    Factors: _____

    Actions: _____

    _____

ACTIVITY 46 **Applying Health Skills**

Avoiding Abuse

Directions ➤ You are a volunteer for a community organization committed to raising public awareness on the topic of preventing and avoiding abuse. Complete the pamphlet below, creating catchy phrases and slogans to relay the Three R's of preventing abuse.

Recognize	Resist	Report

CHAPTER **14** Study Guide

STUDY TIPS
- Read the Health Concepts for each lesson.
- Look up the meanings of any Health Terms that are unfamiliar.
- Read the questions below before you read the chapter.

Directions ➤ As you read the chapter, answer the following questions. Later you can use this guide to review the information in the chapter.

LESSON 1

1. Define the following types of conflicts.

a) Interpersonal conflicts: _____

_____

b) Internal conflicts: _____

2. Name two ways in which conflicts escalate.

_____

3. Write three questions you can ask yourself to help identify the source of a conflict.

_____

_____

_____

_____

_____

_____

LESSON 2

4. What is the term for the process of ending a conflict by cooperating and problem solving together?

_____

5. Identify each of the following.

a) "Three C's" of conflict resolution: _____

b) "Three R's" of conflict resolution: _____

6. Explain how tolerance helps prevent conflict.

_____

_____

7. Define *negotiation*.

_____

_____

8. How does mediation differ from resolving a conflict on one's own?

_____

_____

LESSON 3

9. How is random violence different from other forms of violence?

_____

10. Define *aggravated assault.*

_____

11. List three factors that affect violence.

_____

12. Name three ways you can help stop violence among teens.

_____

_____

_____

_____

LESSON 4

13. Explain the following kinds of abuse.

a) Physical abuse: _____

b) Sexual assault: _____

14. Define *rape.*

_____

15. Name the "three R's" for preventing abuse.

_____

_____

CHAPTER 15 Vocabulary

epidermis	cartilage	skeletal muscles
dermis	ossification	flexors
melanin	ligaments	extensors
athlete's foot	tendons	cardiac muscle
axial skeleton	repetitive motion	muscle tone
appendicular	injury	tendinitis
skeleton	smooth muscles	hernia

Directions ➤ Analyzing the parts that make up a word can help you determine the meaning of the whole word. For example, if you know the meanings of the word parts *osteo-*, *arthr-*, and *-itis*, then you can determine that the word *osteoarthritis* means "disease involving inflammation of bones and joints." Using a good dictionary, analyze the parts of each word and phrase listed above. (Be aware of spelling changes when word parts are combined.) Then answer the questions that follow.

1. The terms *tendon* and *tendinitis* are related. Define the term *tendinitis* using the meaning of *-itis*.

   _____

2. Give the meaning of each part of the following words and the meaning of the word as a whole.

   a) Ossification: _____

   _____

   b) Appendicular: _____

   _____

3. The terms *epidermis* and *dermis* share the same root. Identify the root, and give its meaning. Then explain the similarity and difference between the terms.

   _____

   _____

   _____

4. What does the suffix *-al* mean? Name two terms from the list that contain this suffix, and give their meanings.

   _____

   _____

   _____

5. Two terms in the list share the suffix *-or*. Identify each term and use its word parts to explain its meaning.

   _____

   _____

   _____

Name _____ Date _____ Class Period _____

Good for What Ails You

Directions ➤ Below are packages from various products used to treat problems of the integu-
mentary system or to maintain its health. For each product, identify the condition
it treats or care it affords, along with a brief description; and any possible risks if
treatment or care is not taken.

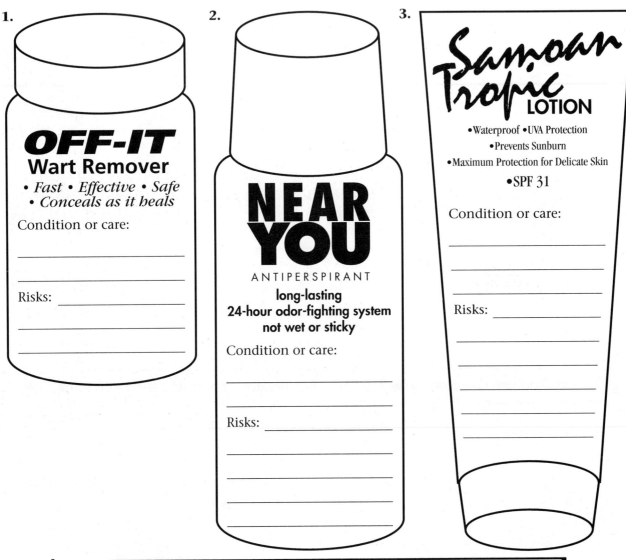

1.

OFF-IT
Wart Remover
• *Fast* • *Effective* • *Safe*
• *Conceals as it heals*

Condition or care:

_____
_____

Risks: _____
_____
_____

2.

NEAR YOU
ANTIPERSPIRANT
**long-lasting
24-hour odor-fighting system
not wet or sticky**

Condition or care:

_____
_____

Risks: _____
_____
_____
_____

3.

Samoan Tropic **LOTION**
•Waterproof •UVA Protection
•Prevents Sunburn
•Maximum Protection for Delicate Skin
•SPF 31

Condition or care:

_____
_____
_____

Risks: _____
_____
_____
_____
_____

4.

ALL CLEAR
THE *ONLY* OINTMENT GUARANTEED TO FIGHT ATHLETE'S FOOT
PROVEN SAFE • HOSPITAL APPROVED • MAXIMUM STRENGTH

Condition or care:

_____
_____

Risks: _____
_____
_____

ACTIVITY 48 Applying Health Skills

E.R.

Directions ➤ You have been asked to help out in the emergency room of a hospital in a ski area during peak skiing season. Below are X rays and charts of several patients. The notes on the charts were penned in by an untrained volunteer. Using the information from the charts and the lesson, answer the questions that follow.

A.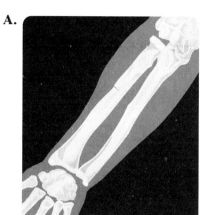

B.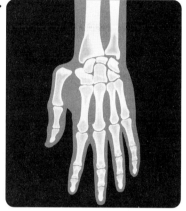

C.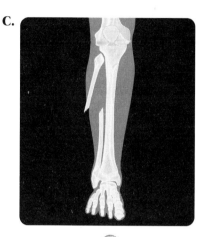

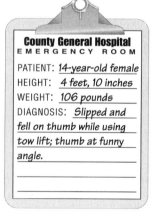

County General Hospital
EMERGENCY ROOM

PATIENT: _26-year-old male_
HEIGHT: _5 feet, 11 inches_
WEIGHT: _163 pounds_
DIAGNOSIS: _Incomplete break of arm bone; no penetration of outer skin._
_____
_____
_____

County General Hospital
EMERGENCY ROOM

PATIENT: _14-year-old female_
HEIGHT: _4 feet, 10 inches_
WEIGHT: _106 pounds_
DIAGNOSIS: _Slipped and fell on thumb while using tow lift; thumb at funny angle._
_____
_____

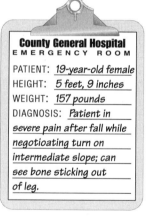

County General Hospital
EMERGENCY ROOM

PATIENT: _19-year-old female_
HEIGHT: _5 feet, 9 inches_
WEIGHT: _157 pounds_
DIAGNOSIS: _Patient in severe pain after fall while negotioating turn on intermediate slope; can see bone sticking out of leg._

1. Which patient has suffered a joint injury? Which type of injury has the person sustained? Which bone is affected?

_____

2. Which of the patients has sustained a hairline fracture? Is the fracture open? Explain your answer.

_____

3. Has any of the patients sustained a fracture that is comminuted? Explain.

_____

_____

4. Which patient may have suffered an injury to the fibula? Explain your answer.

_____

_____

| ACTIVITY **49** | **Applying Health Skills** | FOR USE WITH
CHAPTER 15, LESSON 3 |

The Doctor Is "In"

Directions ➤ Dr. Lovejoy, who specializes in problems of the muscular system, needs your help. Below are notes on the condition of several current patients. For each patient, write a possible diagnosis identifying the problem or injury, and the treatment or lifestyle change called for.

1. Patient, a 16-year-old male, sustained injury of leg playing touch football. Experiencing tenderness in connective tissue and difficulty moving attached muscle. Reports having taken mild pain reliever prior to office visit.

   Possible Diagnosis: _____

   Treatment or Lifestyle Change: _____

   _____

   _____

2. Patient is 3-year-old female. Parents concerned over fact that child is not yet walking; having difficulty raising head or performing simplest movements involving skeletal muscles.

   Possible Diagnosis: _____

   Treatment or Lifestyle Change: _____

   _____

   _____

3. Patient is 48-year-old male reporting abdominal cramps. Physical examination reveals slight protrusion in area of abdomen. Patient's occupation is piano mover.

   Possible Diagnosis: _____

   Treatment or Lifestyle Change: _____

   _____

   _____

4. Patient is 24-year-old female, who leads very active lifestyle—plays tennis, swims, runs. After recent strenuous workout on exercise bicycle at health club, patient experienced painful sensation in left thigh muscle. Pain becomes more intense when leg is stretched or extended.

   Possible Diagnosis: _____

   Treatment or Lifestyle Change: _____

   _____

   _____

CHAPTER **15** **Study Guide**

STUDY TIPS
- Read the Health Concepts for each lesson.
- Look up the meanings of any Health Terms that are unfamiliar.
- Read the questions below before you read the chapter.

Directions ➤ As you read the chapter, answer the following questions. Later you can use this guide to review the information in the chapter.

LESSON 1

1. Name two functions of the skin.

   _____

   _____

2. What are the two main layers of the skin?

   _____

3. Identify two personal habits that promote healthy skin.

   _____

4. Describe the following problems of the skin.

   a) Ringworm: _____

   b) Warts: _____

   c) Corn: _____

LESSON 2

5. Which bones are contained in each of the following?

   a) Axial skeleton: _____

   _____

   b) Appendicular skeleton: _____

   _____

6. What are the four types of bones?

   _____

7. Define *cartilage*.

   _____

8. What are the four types of joints?

   _____

9. Identify two potential problems of each of the following.

   a) Bones: _____

   b) Joints: _____

10. What is repetitive motion injury? What causes it?

_____

_____

LESSON 3

11. Identify two functions of the muscular system.

_____

_____

12. Describe the two complementary actions used by muscles to function.

_____

_____

13. Name the three types of muscles.

_____

_____

14. What are two measures you can take to maintain muscle tone?

_____

_____

15. Identify three injury-related problems of the muscular system.

_____

_____

CHAPTER 16 Vocabulary

neurons	epilepsy	gonads
cerebrum	cerebral palsy	thyroid gland
cerebellum	endocrine glands	parathyroid glands
brain stem	hormones	adrenal glands
reflex	pituitary gland	pancreas

I. Directions ➤ Complete the following passage by writing a term from the list above in each blank.

The _____—the largest, most complex part of the brain—is where most
(1)
conscious activities take place. The second largest part, the _____, is
(2)
concerned mainly with maintaining balance and coordinating skeletal muscle movement. The

_____ is a stalk of nerve cells and fibers that connects the spinal cord to the
(3)
rest of the brain. _____ carry signals from sense receptors to the central
(4)
nervous system (CNS) and from the CNS to muscles and glands. Damage to the brain can result in

_____—a disorder of the nervous system characterized by seizures—or
(5)
_____—a group of nonprogressive neurological disorders.
(6)

II. Directions ➤ Match each endocrine structure in the list above with its descriptive phrase below.

_____   **1.** Ductless, or tubeless, structures that secrete hormones

_____   **2.** The "master gland"

_____   **3.** Glands consisting of two parts whose names are also structures of
                                      the brain

_____   **4.** Gland that serves another body system besides the endocrine
                                      system

_____   **5.** Gland that produces thyroxine

_____   **6.** Smallest glands of the endocrine system

ACTIVITY 50 **Applying Health Skills**   FOR USE WITH
                                                           CHAPTER 16, LESSON 1

Jangled Nerves

Directions ➤ Consuela, a first-year medical student, had just finished studying for her big test in Human Anatomy 101 when she collided with another student on her way out of the library. Now her notes lay scattered on the ground in front of her. Help Consuela re-order her notes on the nervous system, which appear on index cards below. Determine the correct order and grouping of the cards. Then, in the space provided below, write the letters of each *trio* of cards that logically belong together. *Hint:* Be careful: The notes can be arranged in only one order!

a. Somatic nervous system

b. cerebrum

c. consists in part of threadlike extension called axon

d. carry impulses at speeds of close to 250 mph

e. two halves, or hemispheres

f. neurons

g. ANS

h. brain

i. one of two main parts of PNS

j. contains two opposing systems—sympathetic n.s., parasympathetic n.s.

k. parts of nervous system where involuntary responses occur

l. equips body for action in case of emergency

1. _____

2. _____

3. _____

4. _____

ACTIVITY 51 Applying Health Skills

On the Ward

Directions ➤ Read the patients' charts below. All have problems relating to the functions and vital processes of the nervous system. Using the information provided, complete each chart.

Patient 1   **Age: 55**   **Sex: Male**

Symptoms and Other Relevant Information: The patient has noticed an increasing inability to control movement in his hands. He has sustained no injury.

Possible Diagnosis: _____

Prognosis for Patient's Future: _____

_____

Patient 2   **Age: 33**   **Sex: Female**

Symptoms and Other Relevant Information: The patient was rushed to the hospital following a car accident. She has been complaining of extreme discomfort and severe pain in her neck and is unable to move her arms or legs. The patient remembers the accident quite clearly and did not lose consciousness at any time.

Possible Diagnosis: _____

Recommended Treatment: _____

_____

Patient 3   **Age: 73**   **Sex: Female**

Symptoms and Other Relevant Information: The patient was brought to the hospital by her son, who reported that his mother's speech has been sounding strange lately. He insists there are days when she does not seem to recognize him. The patient's coordination is also off.

Possible Diagnosis: _____

Recommended Treatment: _____

_____

Patient 4   **Age: 4**   **Sex: Female**

Symptoms and Other Relevant Information: Parents said the patient was playing quietly when her whole body suddenly seemed to go stiff. She collapsed to the floor and began to shake violently. The incident lasted only a couple of minutes, and when it was over, the patient did not seem to remember any of it. Patient was born six weeks premature after her mother fell down a flight of stairs.

Possible Diagnosis: _____

Possible Cause of Condition: _____

_____

ACTIVITY 52 Applying Health Skills

The Show Must Go On

Directions ➤ Below is the first draft of a script from a scene of a popular TV soap opera set in a hospital. The script contains gaps to be filled in by the show's technical adviser, who has been unavoidably detained. Help the show's production crew get the script ready for rehearsal by filling in the gaps. Write the appropriate word or phrase on the corresponding numbered line following the script.

Scene II.

[The office of Dr. Brent Kimmel. Sinister-sounding music. Kimmel is seated behind his desk when the door opens. His receptionist ushers in the mother of a patient.]

Kimmel *[Gravely.]:* Come in, Mrs. Parker. I've examined your son, and I'm afraid the news is—well, not good. There seems to be a problem with his _____ , also known as the "master gland." This structure, which is the size of a _____ , regulates and controls the
_____ —or at least that's what happens when the gland functions normally. *[Dramatic chord of organ music.]*

(1) ... (2) ... (3)

Mrs. Parker *[Gasping as she holds her hand to her mouth.]:* Oh, no, doctor—you mean . . .

Kimmel *[More gravely still.]:* Yes, Mrs. Parker. I'm afraid Johnny's entire _____ system has gone haywire. There is no telling what may happen! *[Dramatic chord of organ music.]*

(4)

Mrs. Parker *[Gasping again.]:* But, doctor, isn't there something you can . . .

Kimmel *[Somewhat less gravely.]:* Do, Mrs. Parker? One possibility would be to administer synthetic forms of the six _____ produced by the affected lobe of the gland. That lobe, the
_____ lobe, is the _____ part of the gland, as its name implies. *[With pointer, indicates diagram of human body on wall.]* It produces chemical substances that control such diverse body functions as cell growth, hair growth, and even the production of _____
in females who have given birth.

(5) ... (6) ... (7) ... (8)

[Suddenly, door of office swings open, and receptionist appears.]

Receptionist *[Voice registering alarm.]:* Doctor, I'm sorry for interrupting, but it's an emergency! Your patient with diabetes mellitus is in the emergency room. Her blood _____ level is very high. She needs a shot of _____ at once! *[Dramatic chord of organ music.]*

(9) ... (10)

1. _____

2. _____

3. _____

4. _____

5. _____

6. _____

7. _____

8. _____

9. _____

10. _____

CHAPTER 16 Study Guide

STUDY TIPS
- Read the Health Concepts for each lesson.
- Look up the meanings of any Health Terms that are unfamiliar.
- Read the questions below before you read the chapter.

Directions ➤ As you read the chapter, answer the following questions. Later you can use this guide to review the information in the chapter.

LESSON 1

1. Name two functions of the nervous system.

_____

_____

_____

2. What are the two main structures of the nervous system?

_____

_____

3. Define *neurons*.

_____

4. What are the two main parts of the central nervous system?

_____

5. What part of the brain is the site of most conscious and intelligent activities?

_____

6. Tell what is done by each subdivision of the peripheral nervous system.

a) Autonomic nervous system: _____

b) Somatic nervous system: _____

LESSON 2

7. Identify two steps you can take in caring for your nervous system.

_____

8. Name two head injuries.

_____

9. Identify and describe two degenerative diseases of the nervous system.

_____

_____

_____

_____

10. What is epilepsy? What causes it?

_____

_____

LESSON 3

11. Define *hormones.*

_____

_____

12. What is the function of the pituitary gland?

_____

_____

13. Which gland produces hormones that regulate metabolism, body heat production, and bone growth?

_____

14. Identify the function of each of the two parts of the adrenal glands.

a) Adrenal cortex: _____

_____

b) Adrenal medulla: _____

15. What is the function of the pancreas?

_____

_____

CHAPTER **17** Vocabulary

plasma	lymph	trachea
hemoglobin	lymphocytes	bronchi
platelets	congenital	larynx
arteries	respiration	pleurisy
capillaries	diaphragm	asthma
veins	pharynx	

Directions ➤ Many of the words in the list above are related in some way. Create categories for as many words as possible. Then develop a heading for each category that illustrates how the words are related. For example, *arteries* might be grouped with other terms under the heading "Types of Blood Vessels." Add your headings to the chart below. Then write words from the list in the appropriate spaces in the chart.

Types of Blood Vessels			
arteries			

ACTIVITY 53 Applying Health Skills

Circulating Rumors

Directions ➤ For a period of a millennium and a half during the Middle Ages, the teachings of the ancient Greek physician Galen of Pergamum (129–199?) dominated medical thought. Though Galen's contributions to our present understanding of human anatomy are undeniable, his anatomical studies—which were based on the dissection of apes—were full of errors. Below is a translation of an excerpt from one of the more than 500 tracts on medicine Galen produced. Read the excerpt. Then answer the questions that follow.

I am now convinced of an error in the assumptions of my predecessors of the past 400 years—viz. [namely], the common belief that the arteries are vehicles deployed by the body for the exclusive transport of air. It is the blood, rather, which is contained by these vessels. Nor do the arteries alone serve in this capacity, but instead vessels called *veins*—the which betray [reveal] an altogether different character [structure] from arteries—may as well be seen to house the blood. It is from the liver, which as I have elsewhere noted is the seat of the entire system of the body's vessels, that the blood moves to the extremes of the body therein to comprise its flesh. . . .

Its [blood's] chief function is to transport the *pneuma* [life spirit] to all body parts. The blood's red coloring itself is derived of [from] the *pneuma*. . . .

The heart organ (which I charge my colleagues not to complicate [confuse] with the great "hairy heart" of the chest cavity) is made in part of valves. . . . Once entering this organ, the blood may move freely between its ventricles by means of the porous wall that separate[s] them.

1. In this tract, Galen corrects a misconception common among physicians of previous generations. What is it?

   _____

2. What organ does Galen mistakenly identify as the "seat" of the vascular system? What do we know today to be the real hub of this system?

   _____

3. What misconception of Galen did the discovery of hemoglobin eventually put to rest?

   _____

4. What might Galen have been referring to when he spoke of a "great 'hairy heart'?"

   _____

5. For over a thousand years after Galen's time, students of anatomy remained ignorant of the fact that blood circulates. Why do you suppose this may have been the case?

   _____

   _____

   _____

ACTIVITY 54 **Applying Health Skills**

In Case

Directions ➤ A clumsy medical student has misplaced sections of his class notes. The notes have to do with case studies relating to problems of the circulatory and lymphatic systems. Help the student study for his exam by completing the information in each case study.

Case study 1

Patient: 11-year-old male.

Symptoms: Sore throat, fever.

Possible Diagnosis: _____

System Involved: _____

Treatment: _____

_____

_____

Case study 2

Patient: 39-year-old pregnant female; occupation: cashier.

Symptoms: Severe pain in legs, especially after long periods of standing at cash register.

Possible Diagnosis: _____

System Involved: _____

Treatment: _____

_____

_____

Case study 3

Patient: 8-year-old female; parents report she is frequently tired. Preliminary blood workup reveals low level of hemoglobin.

Symptoms: Fatigue.

Possible Diagnosis: _____

System Involved: _____

Treatment: _____

_____

_____

ACTIVITY 55 **Applying Health Skills**

Not Fit to Print

Directions ➤ A local newspaper publishes a weekly medical advice column in which readers' letters about health conditions are answered by a resident physician. Unfortunately, the manuscript pages containing the doctor's answers to this week's questions have been misplaced, and the paper is due to go to press any minute now. You can save the day by answering the letters below. In your answer, identify the likely cause of the problem described, give a brief definition of that problem, and tell what actions the writer can and should take.

1. Dear Doctor:

I suffer from regular headaches that are almost like the constant beating of a drum just behind my eyes. Right now I have a cold, and the pain is almost unbearable. Along with the fever I'm running and my stuffy nose, I feel like just crawling under the covers and staying there until the winter's over. I have to go to work though to earn a living. Isn't there something you can recommend to help stop the headaches?

Yours truly,
In Distress

Dear "In":

_____

_____

_____

_____

_____

2. Dear Doctor:

My eight-year-old son has been wheezing and coughing on and off now for several months. His symptoms are especially severe when I smoke. Last night he gave us a real scare. He woke up around 3:00 in the morning and claimed he was having trouble breathing. His breath was coming in short puffs. At first, I thought he just had a case of the flu, but now my husband and I are convinced it is something more serious. Can you tell me what is wrong?

Yours,
A Concerned Mom

Dear Concerned:

_____

_____

_____

_____

CHAPTER **17** Study Guide

STUDY TIPS
- Read the Health Concepts for each lesson.
- Look up the meanings of any Health Terms that are unfamiliar.
- Read the questions below before you read the chapter.

Directions ➤ As you read the chapter, answer the following questions. Later you can use this guide to review the information in the chapter.

LESSON 1

1. The heart and blood make up two parts of the circulatory system. What is the third part?

   _____

2. Define each of the following parts of blood.

   a) Plasma: _____

   b) Hemoglobin: _____

   c) Platelets: _____

3. Identify the type of blood vessel that fits each of the following descriptions.

   a) The vessels that carry blood away from the heart: _____

   b) The vessels that carry blood between arterioles and small vessels called venules:

   _____

   c) The vessels that return deoxygenated blood to the heart from the body's organs and tissues:

   _____

4. Name the two functions of the lymphatic system.

   _____

5. What are lymphocytes?

   _____

LESSON 2

6. Name two ways you can take care of your circulatory system.

   _____

7. Define *congenital*.

   _____

8. Give two examples of congenital heart disease.

   _____

   _____

9. Name three other circulatory system problems.

_____

_____

10. Name two lymphatic system problems.

_____

_____

LESSON 3

11. Explain respiration, the main function of the respiratory system.

_____

_____

12. Which muscle separates the chest and abdominal cavities, making respiration possible?

_____

13. Define each of the following structures of the respiratory system.

a) Pharynx: _____

b) Trachea: _____

c) Bronchi: _____

14. Give two ways that you can take care of your respiratory system.

_____

_____

15. Define each of the following respiratory problems.

a) Asthma: _____

_____

b) Pleurisy: _____

_____

CHAPTER 18 Vocabulary

digestion	bile	ureters
absorption	indigestion	bladder
elimination	hiatal hernia	urethra
ingestion	appendicitis	cystitis
mastication	peptic ulcer	urethritis
peristalsis	urine	incontinence
gastric juices	nephrons	hemodialysis
chyme		

Directions ➤ Analyzing the parts that make up a word can help you determine the meaning of the whole word. For example, if you know the meanings of the word parts *dys-*, *peps-* and *-ic,* then you can determine that the word *dyspeptic* means "having poor digestion or suffering from indigestion." Using a good dictionary, analyze the parts of each word and phrase listed above. (Be aware of spelling changes when word parts are combined.) Then answer the questions that follow.

1. Give the meaning of each part of the word *hemodialysis* and the meaning of the word as a whole.

_____

_____

2. Locate two words in the list with the prefix *in-*. Write the words and explain how the prefix affected the meanings of the words.

_____

_____

_____

3. Three terms in the list share the root *-itis.* Identify each term and use its word parts to explain its meaning.

_____

_____

_____

4. Which terms in the list share the Latin root *urin-* (or *ur-*)? Identify the terms and explain how they are related.

_____

_____

_____

ACTIVITY 56 Applying Health Skills

Incredible Journey

Directions ➤ The date is sometime in the future. You are part of a scientific team that has been shrunk to the size of a pinhead. You have just completed a mission through a human digestive system in a vessel specially designed to withstand the chemical actions. Below are one team member's log entries for the six-day journey. Unfortunately, the log entries have become jumbled. Determine the correct order for the entries, and write the proper number for the day in the space provided before each entry. Then rewrite the entry, using the correct names of organs and processes of digestion to explain what is happening.

Day _____ : WE ARE IN A LARGE CAVERN. THIS SEEMS TO BE A STORAGE CENTER FOR FOOD. AT THE BOTTOM OF THE CAVERN IS A POOL OF LIQUID THAT APPEARS TO BE BOILING. I WONDER WHAT IT IS?

_____

_____

Day _____ : THE RELATIVELY UNDIGESTED FOOD IS BEING CONVERTED INTO A SOLUTION THROUGH A SECRETION OF SOME KIND OF LIQUID. THE CHEMICAL SENSORS ON THE OUTSIDE OF OUR VESSEL REVEAL THIS LIQUID TO BE LARGELY WATER.

_____

_____

_____

Day _____ : THE TWISTING, WINDING PASSAGE WE ARE IN IS LINED WITH FINGERLIKE PROJECTIONS. WE ARE EXPERIENCING MORE OF THOSE EARTHQUAKE-LIKE TREMORS.

_____

_____

Day _____ : WE JUST PASSED THE LIPS. TWO ROWS OF HUGE WHITE TABLETS—ONE ABOVE, ONE BELOW—ARE CRUSHING RECENTLY EATEN FOOD. OUR VESSEL IS MOVING ALONG ON A SOFT, PINK VELVETLIKE MAT, WHICH IS FORMING THE FOOD INTO A BALL.

_____

_____

_____

Day _____ : WE HAVE JUST PASSED A FLAP OF SKIN CLOSING OFF ONE OF TWO STEEP, DARK TUNNELS. WE ARE NOW HEADING DOWN THE TUNNEL THAT HAS REMAINED OPEN. OUR VESSEL IS BEING ROCKED BY A WAVE OF EARTHQUAKE-LIKE CONTRACTIONS.

_____

_____

Day _____ : THE TUNNEL WE ARE CURRENTLY PASSING THROUGH SEEMS TO BE REMOVING WATER FROM THE DIGESTED FOOD. OUR CHEMICAL SENSORS REPORT THAT THERE ARE BACTERIA IN THE VICINITY.

_____

_____

CHAPTER 18 Study Guide

STUDY TIPS
- Read the Health Concepts for each lesson.
- Look up the meanings of any Health Terms that are unfamiliar.
- Read the questions below before you read the chapter.

Directions ➤ As you read the chapter, answer the following questions. Later you can use this guide to review the information in the chapter.

LESSON 1

1. What role do the teeth play in the digestive process?

   _____

   _____

2. What is the name for the involuntary muscular contractions that move food through the esophagus?

   _____

3. List the main digestive activities that take place in the stomach.

   _____

   _____

   _____

4. Explain how each part of gastric juices aids in digestion.

   a) Pepsin: _____

   _____

   b) Hydrochloric acid: _____

   _____

5. What are the three parts of the small intestine? Which of these parts does chyme enter after leaving the stomach?

   _____

   _____

6. What are the main functions of the large intestine?

   _____

   _____

LESSON 2

7. Explain how indigestion and heartburn are different.

   _____

   _____

8. Define *hiatal hernia.*

_____

_____

9. Identify three other functional problems of the digestive system.

_____

_____

10. Identify each of the following structural digestive system problems.

a) The formation of small crystals in the gallbladder: _____

b) A sore in the lining of the digestive tract: _____

LESSON 3

11. What is the chief function of the urinary system?

_____

_____

12. What is the function of the kidneys?

_____

_____

_____

13. Define each of the following tubes that lead to or from the bladder.

a) Ureters: _____

b) Urethra: _____

14. Identify symptoms of each of the following problems of the urinary system.

a) Cystitis: _____

_____

b) Urethritis: _____

_____

15. Name three kidney problems.

_____

_____

CHAPTER 19 Vocabulary

testosterone	circumcision	fallopian tubes
sperm	sterility	zygote
testes	ova	uterus
penis	vagina	cervix
semen	ovaries	menstrual cycle
fertilization	ovulation	infertility

Directions ➤ Etymology, the study of a word's origins, can provide clues to the meanings of an entire family of words and phrases. Using a dictionary that contains the etymology of words, investigate the origins of each word and phrase listed above. Then answer the questions that follow.

1. Whic_ _ms in the list come from a Latin word that means "egg"?

   _____

2. Two terms i_ _ list come from words that mean "seed," but they are of different origins. Identify each term and _ 'anguage from which it derives.

   _____   _____

3. One term in the list s_ _ s common roots with the dictionary entries circumference and incision. Identify the term and it_ _mology. Explain why its origin is appropriate to its current meaning in English.

   _____   _____
   _____   _____
   _____   _____
   _____   _____

4. Two of the terms can be traced to a Latin wor_ _ning "witness." Which terms are they? Identify at least three other dictionary entries that have _ same etymology.

   Terms from list: _____   _____

   Dictionary entries with the same etymology: _____   _____

   _____   _____

5. One of the terms in the list is an eponym, a term derived from _ name of a person. Identify the term and its etymology.

   _____
   _____

6. Which term in the list comes from a Latin term meaning "month," from wh_ _ the word moon is also derived? Explain why the connection between this term and moon is appropriate.

   _____
   _____

ACTIVITY 59 **Applying Health Skills**

A "Page" from the Book on Reproductive Health

Directions ➤ You are the administrator of a web site titled "The Help Page." The site dispenses medical advice to individuals who send in problems by e-mail. Today's special topic is care and problems of the male reproductive system. Read each e-mail message, and decide whether a problem exists. Indicate also what measures, including seeing a doctor, each correspondent should take.

1. Hi. I'm Rob and I just turned 19. I'm a freshman in college where I'm a member of the weight-lifting team. For the past few months, I've been working my abs (abdominal muscles) pretty hard in preparation for a competition that's coming up. In the last week, I've started noticing some pain in my gut. I'm hoping this is just "nerves" over the competition, but I want to make sure.

—rob_e@univ.smallville.edu

TO: rob_e@univ.smallville.edu

_____

_____

_____

2. I just celebrated my fifty-fifth birthday. My most recent checkup was about six months ago, and everything checked out normal. Recently, however, I started having problems when I urinate. My wife thinks I should go back to the doctor. What do you think?

—harry177@for.the.people.com

TO: harry177@for.the.people.com

_____

_____

_____

3. I'm writing you because my husband is too embarrassed to take action for what I think might be a serious problem. Rudy is a 31-year-old male construction worker. For the past couple of months, he has had this dull ache in his lower abdomen. Last week, while showering, he also noticed that one of his testicles seemed to be larger than usual. He says he probably just pulled a muscle at work. Is he right? Please don't mention his name in your reply.

—consco@hpes.com

TO: consco@hpes.com

_____

_____

_____

ACTIVITY 61 **Applying Health Skills**

Letter Imperfect

Directions ➤ The following is a personal letter written by a mother-to-be who, regrettably, is not as prepared for the responsibilities of pregnancy as she should be. Read the letter, underlining every sentence that reveals a poor or wrong decision on the writer's part. Then answer the questions that follow.

Hi, Sis!

Ted and I are really excited at the prospect of being someone's daddy and mommy. You should see the way Ted is fawning all over me! Last night at 11:30, he went out in the pouring rain to get me cigarettes and candy. He's going to be a terrific father.

As you know, Mom has been on my case now for three months to see the doctor even though I feel great. People of our parents' generation sure have some oldfangled ideas! Do you remember Mom telling me back when I first found out I was pregnant that you could actually have a *midwife* deliver your baby? What century is she living in?

Anyway, Ted, Jr., is doing fine. The doctor did a sonogram—you know, a picture of my womb—and said the baby is around 14 inches long. We have the picture, and is it cute—little Teddy is sucking his thumb!

I'm going to have to cut this letter short, Sis. I've got another headache and have to go take something. Don't tell Mom I've been having headaches. If she finds out, she'll start hounding me to call the doctor—as if I need his permission to take an aspirin!

I'll write again soon.

Love,
Carla

1. At what stage of pregnancy is Carla? How can you tell?

_____

_____

2. Is Carla getting proper prenatal care? Explain your answer.

_____

_____

_____

3. What misconception does Carla have about health care professionals?

_____

_____

4. Based on Carla's personal habits, what serious health risks may her fetus be facing?

_____

_____

_____

ACTIVITY 62 Applying Health Skills

Ask Inge

Directions ➤ Inge, who writes a newspaper advice column, has received a number of letters addressing aspects of heredity. Help Inge answer the letters. Using information from the lesson, respond to each writer.

1. Dear Inge:

Because my husband's grandmother and a great aunt had cystic fibrosis, we were concerned that our baby might, too. Happily, our new baby daughter is just the most perfect thing you have ever seen. Now if only I could get my sister to stop nagging me about taking the baby to a doctor. She's obviously healthy. Any suggestions for an overbearing relative?

—Perfectly Pleased

Dear Perfectly:

_____

_____

_____

_____

2. Dear Inge:

My mother and father both have brown eyes, and so does my brother. My eyes are blue. The only conclusion I can draw is that I'm adopted. How can I go about tracing my real parents?

—Adopted in Kansas

Dear Adopted:

_____

_____

_____

_____

3. Dear Inge:

My husband, Tom, and I are now expecting our third child. Tom says that if this child is not a boy, it is my fault. What do I tell him?

—Mother of Two and a Half

Dear Mother:

_____

_____

_____

_____

ACTIVITY 63 **Applying Health Skills**

Next Caller

Directions ➤ A popular call-in TV program has invited an expert on childhood develo nt to field phone calls. That expert is *you*. Below are problems two of the callers expe-riencing with their children. Respond to each caller, being sure to me n the developmental tasks involved in each situation.

Phone call from Dorie of Midville:

"My daughter Alfreda, who is three, insists on dressing herself each morning. I am as eage ny-one for her to become self-sufficient, but lately I've been losing patience. I have a job to get d I just can't wait around all morning. My husband says my scolding is harming our child. Don think he's just making a mountain out of a molehill and that Alfreda will turn out fine?"

Your response: _____

_____

_____

_____

_____

_____

Phone call from Allan J. of Center City:

"I'd like to know why kids are such slobs these days. Take my son, who just turned eigh recently discovered the joys of making model sports cars out of kits. What he hasn't discovered is to clean up after himself. Day in and day out his mother and I try to impress upon him the imp nce of cleaning up the little bits of plastic and glue, and the other messes he makes. All that hap , though, is that he looks at us with these sad, puppy-dog eyes. It's as if he hasn't heard a word we aid! How can we get through to him?"

Your response: _____

_____

_____

_____

_____

_____

CHAPTER 20 Study Guide

STUDY TIPS
- Read the Concepts to Learn for each lesson.
- Look up unfamiliar words in the Terms to Learn.
- Read the questions below before you read the chapter.

Directions ➤ As you read the chapter, answer the following questions. Later you can use this guide to review the information in the chapter.

LESSON 1

1. Explain how each of the following provides support to a growing embryo:

   a) Placenta. _____

   _____

   b) Umbilical cord. _____

   _____

2. What is the relationship between the terms *fetus* and *embryo*?

   _____

   _____

3. Identify two components of prenatal care.

   _____

   _____

   _____

4. Identify two substances that, when taken into a pregnant female's body, can place her unborn child at risk.

   _____

5. Identify the three stages of birth.

   a) Stage One: _____

   b) Stage Two: _____

   c) Stage Three: _____

6. Explain the differences between a miscarriage and a stillbirth.

   _____

   _____

LESSON 2

7. Explain the relationship between chromosomes and genes.

   _____

   _____

8. What is the difference between dominant and recessive genes?

_____

_____

_____

9. Explain the role of X and Y chromosomes in determining gender.

_____

_____

_____

10. What is a genetic disorder?

_____

_____

11. Define each of the following methods used to identify genetic disorders.

a) Amniocentesis: _____

_____

b) Ultrasound: _____

_____

c) Chorionic villi sampling: _____

_____

LESSON 3

12. Define *developmental task.*

_____

_____

13. Name the first four stages of growth and development advanced by psychologist Erik Erikson.

_____

_____

14. What is autonomy? During what stage of development does autonomy occur?

_____

_____

15. Identify two physical skills acquired during late childhood. Identify two social skills.

_____

_____

_____

CHAPTER **21** Vocabulary

adolescence	cognition	priorities
puberty	personal identity	self-control
sex characteristics	abstinence	sexually transmitted
gametes		disease (STD)

Directions ➤ Use the clues to solve the puzzle. Write one letter of each answer in the space provided. Copy the boxed letters in order to the spaces at the bottom of the page to spell out a phrase that represents something every teen should hope to become.

1. Traits related to one's gender
2. Reproductive cells produced by the gonads
3. Things that are first in importance
4. The act or process of knowing
5. The conscious decision to avoid harmful behaviors
6. The period of time when males and females become physically able to reproduce
7. The factors you believe make you unique
8. The stage between childhood and adulthood
9. An infectious disease spread through sexual contact
10. A person's ability to use responsibility to override emotions

1. _ _ _ _ _ ☐☐_ _ _ ☐_ _ _ _ _ _ _
2. _ _ _ _ _ _ ☐
3. ☐_ _ _ _ _ _ _ _ _
4. _ ☐_ _ _ _ _ _ ☐
5. _ _ ☐_ ☐_ _ _ _ _
6. _ _ ☐_ _ _ _
7. _ _ _ _ _ _ _ ☐_ _ ☐_ _ _ _ _
8. ☐☐_ _ _ _ _ _ _ _ _
9. _ _ _ ☐_ _ ☐_ _ _ _ _ _ _ _ _ _ _ _ _
   _ _ _ _ _ _ _
10. _ _ _ _ _ _ _☐_ _ _

I will become _____ .

ACTIVITY 64 **Applying Health Skills**

A Penny for Their Thoughts

Directions ➤ Have you ever wondered what it would be like to be able to read another person's mind? Here is your big chance. The thought balloons below reveal the innermost thoughts and longings of students at Midville High. Read the contents of the balloons. Then identify one developmental task of adolescence the thinker has met and one the thinker has yet to meet.

1. *Connie, studying appearance critically in full length mirror.*

   I wish I'd start looking more grown up. Well, I'd better stop wishing and get busy making that costume I promised to sew for my little sister's school play.

   Developmental task Connie has met:

   _____

   Developmental task she has yet to meet:

   _____

2. *Kareem, sitting in room, reflecting on day.*

   I've thought long and hard over whether to report Rod for cheating on the history exam. I'm going to speak with Rod and encourage him to do the right thing. First, I have to go speak to Mom about straightening up my room— it's a mess!

   Developmental task Kareem has met:

   _____

   Developmental task Kareem has yet to meet:

   _____

3. *Carlos, seated at desk in room, grinning.*

   I sure had fun today putting that whoopee cushion on Martha's chair in math class; man, was she ever ticked off!

   Turns to "To Do" list on desk before him.

   Now down to business: Tomorrow I want to talk to the guidance counselor about what courses I can take next year to help prepare me for med school.

   Developmental task Carlos has met:

   _____

   Developmental task Carlos has yet to meet:

   _____

ACTIVITY 65 **Applying Health Skills**

Growth Fund

Directions ➤ Imagine that there is a special "growth fund" in which a person could make deposits that would enable that person to make responsible decisions while growing to maturity. The questions that follow constitute a growth fund of sorts. Fill in each item in the space provided. Use a separate sheet of paper if you need additional space.

1. Choose priorities in life:

a) _____

b) _____

c) _____

2. Values that are important to consider:

_____

_____

3. Resources available to discuss feelings and concerns:

_____

_____

_____

4. High-pressure situations that may arise:

_____

_____

_____

5. Ways of saying no when being pressured to do something against a person's values:

_____

_____

_____

6. Ways in which a decision could be harmful:

_____

_____

_____

CHAPTER 21 **Study Guide**

STUDY TIPS
- Read the Health Concepts for each lesson.
- Look up the meanings of any Health Terms that are unfamiliar.
- Read the questions below before you read the chapter.

Directions ➤ As you read the chapter, answer the following questions. Later you can use this guide to review the information in the chapter.

LESSON 1

1. What is a term for the stage of life between childhood and adulthood?

_____

2. What is puberty?

_____

_____

3. Give two examples of secondary sex characteristics that occur in males and two that occur in females during puberty.

_____

_____

_____

4. What is another term for reproductive cells produced by the gonads?

_____

5. Name two changes that occur in adolescents during puberty in each of the following areas.

   a) Mental changes: _____

   _____

   _____

   b) Social changes: _____

   _____

6. List three developmental tasks basic to adolescence.

_____

_____

_____

_____

_____

7. What is a personal identity?

_____

_____

8. Write three questions you can ask yourself as you form a personal identity.

_____

_____

_____

_____

_____

LESSON 2

9. Define *abstinence.*

_____

_____

10. What are priorities? Identify two priorities in life that can help a teen make the choice for abstinence.

_____

_____

11. What are three ways of steering clear of high-pressure situations once you have chosen to be abstinent?

_____

_____

12. Define *self-control.*

_____

_____

13. Name four consequences of sexual activity for teens.

_____

_____

14. What potential problems does an unwanted pregnancy pose for teens?

_____

_____

15. Define *sexually transmitted disease.*

_____

_____

_____

CHAPTER 22 Vocabulary

physical maturity	marital adjustment	generativity
emotional maturity	planned pregnancy	menopause
emotional intimacy	self-directed	empty-nest syndrome
commitment	transitions	integrity

Directions ➤ An analogy compares two words or ideas in a way that shows some similarity or relationship between them. An *analogy sentence* is an analogy in which one of the terms is missing and must be inferred. For example, in the analogy sentence *word is to sentence as* _____ *is to article*, the missing term, *paragraph*, might be arrived at using the following logic: "In just the way words make up sentences, so paragraphs make up articles." Complete each analogy sentence below by writing one of the words or phrases from the above list.

1. autonomy is to early childhood as _____ is to middle adulthood

2. physical maturity is to body as _____ is to feelings

3. _____ is to responsibility as unplanned pregnancy is to irresponsibility

4. caring is to _____ as indifference is to emotional distance

5. doctor and lawyer are to careers as graduation and marriage are to _____

6. _____ is to menstruation as adulthood is to adolescence

7. faithlessness is to loyalty as disloyalty is to _____

8. independent is to _____ as dependent is to other-directed

9. _____ is to developmental task as empty-nest syndrome is to transition

10. sharing is to _____ as instilling values is to parenthood

11. vegetable is to ripeness as human body is to _____

ACTIVITY 66 **Applying Health Skills**

The Coming of Age of Randy Burston

Directions ➤ Below are partial notes for a screenplay for an upcoming film titled *The Coming of Age of Randy Burston*. The movie chronicles the adventures of a young male. Read the notes. Then answer the questions that follow.

As the film opens, we see Randy seated on a train rumbling through the countryside. It is the fall of the year after Randy has graduated from college, and he is on his way to the big city, where he has accepted a job in accounting.

As Randy leans back in his seat, he closes his eyes. We flash back to him out on a date with Alexa, his high school sweetheart in the small town where he grew up. The scene shows the two promising to be together always, then cuts suddenly to the present. Randy looks at the empty seat next to him on the train, smiles, and shakes his head.

Randy reaches into his knapsack and pulls out a photo of his family on vacation in Maine. It was taken the year Randy was 12. As he gazes at the photo, he is transported back to that scene. Individuals in the photo spring to life. Randy overhears his mother telling his sister, who is older, about the importance of leaving a mark on society.

A shrill blast of the train's whistle jostles Randy back to the present. The train is headed through a tunnel, and Randy is able to glimpse his reflection in the window—he sees his squared jaw and other "manly" features.

1. What evidence do you have that Randy Burston may have reached physical maturity?

   _____

   _____

2. Which developmental tasks of adulthood has Randy satisfied? Explain your answers.

   _____

   _____

   _____

3. Which developmental task of adulthood might Randy's mother have been hinting at in her conversation in Maine with Randy's older sister? What are some ways of achieving this task?

   _____

   _____

4. Do you think Randy has achieved emotional maturity? Why or why not?

   _____

   _____

ACTIVITY 67 Applying Health Skills

Learned Counsel

Directions ➤ Read each statement below. Then (a) identify the problem and (b) indicate what measures family members need to take to resolve it.

1. Before we got married, Ernesto and I never talked about having a baby. We both wanted to finish school and get settled in jobs first. Well, we've done that. I'm ready to have a baby now, but whenever I try to talk to Ernesto about it, he ignores me, changes the subject, or walks out.

   Problem: _____

   Possible solution: _____
   _____

2. I don't know what to do any more. Donald is driving me crazy. Yesterday, he scribbled all over the dining room wall with crayons. The day before that, he rode his bicycle into my favorite floor lamp and broke it. I told him he would really be in trouble when his father got home, but Donald didn't even seem to hear me. He never seems to hear me, no matter how loud I scream.

   Problem: _____
   _____

   Possible solution: _____
   _____
   _____

3. Although everybody said it wouldn't work, Joe and I eloped when we were eighteen. At first it seemed as though we would prove everybody wrong. Now, a year later, things have changed. Joe gets angry when the phone rings and it's one of my old friends. What's so terrible if I just keep up on who's dating whom? I'm confused—and depressed.

   Problem: _____
   _____
   _____

   Possible solution: _____
   _____

4. My husband works very hard and spends most of his day at the office. He has very little time to spend with our three children. Whenever I mention it to him, he gets angry. He says he's trying to give them the best of everything and I should want that, too.

   Problem: _____

   Possible solution: _____
   _____

ACTIVITY 68 Applying Health Skills

Just the Facts

Directions ➤ Elm Street is a typical street. Below are facts about five of its residents—Ms. Gallo, Mr. Fidditch, Mrs. O'Flaherty, Mr. Jefferson, and Ms. Schulz. The facts are incomplete, however. Using the available information, as well as information from the lesson on the aging experience, determine the address, stage of adulthood, and parental status (whether the individual is a parent) of each resident. Complete the chart at the bottom of the page as you sort out the facts.

- Each of the five residents lives at one of the following addresses: 228, 233, 236, 239, 241.

- This resident of Elm Street is the father of two grown children.

- Mr. Jefferson and his wife are childless.

- The resident at No. 236, a female, is suffering from empty-nest syndrome.

- In recent years, Mr. Fidditch's attention has begun shifting away from himself and toward concerns for future generations.

- The resident at No. 239 has succeeded at the developmental task of generativity.

- Ms. Gallo enjoys frequent visits with her grandchildren and is able to look back on her life with feelings of wholeness and contentment.

- The resident of the house with the lowest address number is undergoing a midlife crisis.

- All the houses are brick except for the one at No. 228.

- The resident at 236 bicycles 3 miles each day.

- Mr. Jefferson's next-door neighbor is currently meeting the developmental task of generativity.

- The resident at No. 241 retired from the workforce 20 years ago.

- The resident of the wood house is an unmarried female who never had children.

	Stage of Adulthood	Address	Parental Status
Ms. Gallo			
Mr. Fidditch			
Mrs. O'Flaherty			
Mr. Jefferson			
Ms. Schulz			

CHAPTER 22 Study Guide

STUDY TIPS
- Read the Concepts to Learn for each lesson.
- Look up the meanings of any Health Terms that are unfamiliar.
- Read the questions below before you read the chapter.

Directions ➤ As you read the chapter, answer the following questions. Later you can use this guide to review the information in the chapter.

LESSON 1

1. Define each of the following terms.

    a) Physical maturity: _____

    _____

    b) Emotional maturity: _____

    _____

2. List three characteristics of an emotionally mature person.

    _____

    _____

3. Name the four life aspects on which the developmental tasks of adulthood are focused.

    _____

    _____

4. What is emotional intimacy?

    _____

    _____

LESSON 2

5. Name three factors that tend to lead to a well-adjusted marriage.

    _____

    _____

    _____

    _____

6. Give two reasons why teen marriages often fail.

    _____

    _____

7. List two common sources of conflict in marriage.

_____

_____

_____

8. Define *planned pregnancy.*

_____

_____

9. Name three responsibilities of parenthood.

_____

_____

10. Define *self-directed.*

_____

_____

_____

LESSON 3

11. What are life transitions?

_____

_____

12. Name and define a developmental task associated with middle adulthood.

_____

_____

13. What is menopause? During what stage of adulthood does it occur?

_____

_____

14. Define *empty-nest syndrome.*

_____

_____

15. Name and define a developmental task associated with late adulthood.

_____

_____

_____

CHAPTER 23 Vocabulary

medicines	synergistic effect	prescription
vaccine	antagonistic	medicines
analgesics	interaction	over-the-counter
side effects	tolerance	(OTC) medicines
additive interaction	withdrawal	medicine misuse

Directions ➤ A number of different relationships exist among words and phrases and the ideas they represent.

- A *hierarchical relationship* is a relationship in which one word is higher in rank than another. Examples: *general → colonel, high → low.*
- A *cause-effect relationship* is a relationship in which a condition or event represented by one word is a possible cause of a condition or event represented by another. Examples: *pathogen → illness, overeating → overweight.*
- An *antonymic relationship* is a relationship in which two or more words are opposite in meaning. Examples: *disease → health, warmth → coolness.*
- A *parallel relationship* is a relationship in which two or more words share an equivalent status. Examples: *tiger → lion, mother → father.*

Use the information on word relationships to answer the questions that follow.

1. Explain the antonymic relationship between the terms *synergistic effect* and *antagonistic interaction.*

   _____

   _____

   _____

2. Explain the cause-effect relationship between the terms *medicines* and *side effects.*

   _____

3. *Antitoxin* is a term from the chapter that has a parallel relationship with one of the terms in the list above. Identify that term and explain the relationship.

   _____

   _____

4. In what way might the terms *prescription medicines* and *over-the-counter (OTC)* medicines be said to exhibit a hierarchical relationship?

   _____

   _____

   _____

5. Identify a term from the list that has a cause-effect relationship with *withdrawal.* Explain that relationship.

   _____

   _____

ACTIVITY 69 **Applying Health Skills**

Disappearing Act

Directions ➤ Ongoing advances in medicine are helping stamp out diseases in both industrialized and developing nations. The facts in the list below, compiled by the World Health Organization (WHO), describe a number of disappearing diseases. Some of these will be familiar to you, and some will not. Select and research two of the diseases mentioned. Then complete the form that follows.

Facts

- Poliomyelitis is targeted for global elimination within the next several years. There are now 145 countries completely free of the disease.

- Leprosy is steadily being defeated and should no longer represent a significant public health problem within the next few years.

- Worldwide cases of guinea-worm disease—*dracunculiasis*—have fallen from 3.5 million in 1986 to about 120,000 in 1995. Only 1 to 4 cases remained in most third-world villages.

- *Onchocerciasis*, or "river blindness," is being eliminated from 11 West African countries.

- Chagas disease is being stamped out in Argentina, Bolivia, Brazil, Chile, Paraguay and Uruguay.

	Disease 1	Disease 2
Name of Disease		
Cause		
Medicine Being Used to Combat/Treat		
1. Category of Medicine		
2. Side Effects		

ACTIVITY 70 Applying Health Skills

What's in a Name?

Directions ➤ Have you ever read the label on a prescription or OTC medicine and wondered about all the complex, multisyllabic words? The passage below sheds some light on why medicine manufacturers include those long strings of letters. Using information from the passage and the lesson, answer the questions that follow.

All medicines generally have three names—a brand name, a generic name, and a chemical name. The *brand name*, which is chosen by the manufacturer, is usually a word that can be easily pronounced, recognized, or remembered. The *generic name* is the official medical name for the medicine's basic active ingredient. The *chemical name* is a technical description of the medicine's makeup. As an example, the brand name of a medicine used to treat conditions related to AIDS is *Retrovir*. The generic name is *zidovudine*. The chemical name is *3-azido-3-deoxythymidine*.

Generic names are a clue to medicines that are in the same chemical family. For example, penicillin and its derivatives—ampicillin, cloxacillin, and methicillin—all end with the suffix *-cillin*. In similar fashion, medicines of the sulfa family—sulfacetamide, sulfamethoxazole, and sulfisoxazone—all contain the root *sulfa*. However, chemical similarity can be misleading when it comes to the medicine's effect and use. Acetaminophen, for example, is an analgesic. Acetazolamide, which begins with the same combining form, *acet-*, is a type of diuretic.

1. Which name of a medicine would be most useful to a pharmacist? Which would be most useful to a physician? Explain your answers.

_____

_____

_____

_____

2. If your doctor gave you a prescription for amoxycillin, to what family of medicines would it belong?

_____

_____

3. Suppose that the label on an OTC medicine contained the following words and phrases: *acetylsalicylide, Pain-Away,* and *analgesic*. Which of these do you think would be the product's generic name? Explain your responses.

_____

_____

4. Do you think the brand name chosen for the product described in the previous question would be a good one? Why or why not?

_____

_____

CHAPTER 23 Study Guide

STUDY TIPS
■ Read the Health Concepts for each lesson.
■ Look up the meanings of any Health Terms that are unfamiliar.
■ Read the questions below before you read the chapter.

Directions ➤ As you read the chapter, answer the following questions. Later you can use this guide to review the information in the chapter

LESSON 1

1. Name three of the four basic categories of medicines.

_____

_____

2. What are vaccines?

_____

_____

3. What are antibiotics and how do they work?

_____

_____

4. What is the name for the group of medicines that relieve pain?

_____

_____

5. Name three kinds of medicines that help the heart and regulate blood pressure.

_____

_____

6. What are side effects of medicines?

_____

_____

7. When does an additive interaction occur?

_____

_____

8. Define *synergistic effect.*

_____

_____

9. Which kind of interaction occurs when the effect of a medicine is canceled or reduced when taken with another medicine?

_____

_____

10. Define each of the following problems that accompany dependence on a particular medicine.

a) Tolerance: _____

_____

b) Withdrawal: _____

_____

LESSON 2

11. What does the Food and Drug Administration (FDA) do?

_____

_____

12. What is the name of the class of medicines that cannot be used safely without the written approval of a licensed physician?

_____

_____

13. Define *over-the-counter medicines.*

_____

_____

14. What is medicine misuse?

_____

_____

15. Give three examples of medicine misuse.

_____

_____

_____

_____

CHAPTER 24 Vocabulary

addiction	carbon monoxide	mainstream smoke
nicotine	smokeless tobacco	sidestream smoke
stimulant	leukoplakia	nicotine withdrawal
tar	passive smoke	nicotine substitutes
carcinogens		

Directions ➤ Analyzing the parts that make up a word can help you determine the meaning of the whole word. For example, if you know the meanings of the word parts *physi-*, *-ology*, and *-al*, then you can determine that the word *physiological* means "of or relating to the study of the functions and activities of life." Using a good dictionary, analyze the parts of each word and phrase listed above. (Be aware of spelling changes when word parts are combined.) Then answer the questions that follow.

1. Give the meaning of each part of the following words and the meaning of each word as a whole.

a) Leukoplakia: _____

b) Carcinogens: _____

c) Addiction: _____

_____

d) Smokeless: _____

_____

e) Withdrawal: _____

_____

2. Parts of two of the terms in the list are compound words, words formed by combining two or more words. Identify the terms and use the meanings of the parts of the compound words to determine the meaning of the words as a whole.

a) _____

_____

b) _____

_____

ACTIVITY **71** Applying Health Skills

Pack of Lies

Directions ➤ Although the advertising of tobacco products on radio and TV was banned in 1971, print advertising was not. Ads for cigarettes, cigars, and other tobacco products continue to appear on billboards and the pages of magazines and newspapers. Many of these ads use deceptive techniques or send hidden messages to make the products seem attractive—and harmless. Below are two typical ads. Examine the ads. Then answer the questions that follow.

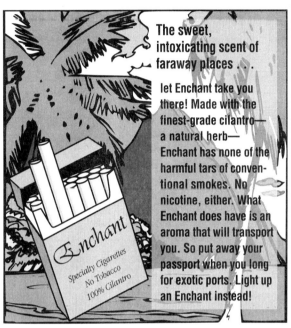

The sweet, intoxicating scent of faraway places . . .

let Enchant take you there! Made with the finest-grade cilantro—a natural herb—Enchant has none of the harmful tars of conventional smokes. No nicotine, either. What Enchant does have is an aroma that will transport you. So put away your passport when you long for exotic ports. Light up an Enchant instead!

Future Hall of Fame pitcher Rollie McDither wouldn't be caught dead on the mound without his Macho™ brand smokeless tobacco.

Says Rollie: "I used to smoke, but smoking's no good for you. That's why I switched to Macho™ brand. A pinch between my cheek and gum, and I'm good for nine innings, without relief." So be like Rollie: Do the smart—the safe—thing. Switch to Macho™ brand.

1. Which of the ads features a celebrity endorsement? At what audience might this ad be targeted?

_____

_____

2. Identify at least one myth or misconception in each ad:

   a) Macho smokeless tobacco: _____

   _____

   _____

   b) Enchant cigarettes: _____

   _____

   _____

3. In what way are the visual images in the two ads deceptive?

_____

_____

_____

_____

ACTIVITY 72 Applying Health Skills

Smokescreen

Directions ➤ Below are remarks you may have heard from people who have not yet managed to kick the tobacco habit. Such people tend to create "smokescreens"—systems of incorrect beliefs or misconceptions—for themselves. For each remark, identify the faulty thinking or misinformation. Then, using information from the lesson, expose the falsehoods stated or implied by the myths.

1. My older brother uses smokeless tobacco. He says that it can't hurt you the way cigarettes, cigars, and pipes can, because when you dip, there's no smoke. I want to be a big man, like my brother. I'm going to use smokeless tobacco when I get bigger.

    Faulty thinking/misinformation: _____

    _____

    Realities: _____

    _____

    _____

2. I don't care what the books say: I enjoy smoking and have no intention of stopping just because I'm expecting my first child in two months. Those studies are just written by a bunch of health nuts anyway!

    Faulty thinking/misinformation: _____

    _____

    Realities: _____

    _____

    _____

3. Everybody is on my case about my smoking—even my eight-year-old. It's always the same message: "You've got to stop smoking. Cigarettes can kill you." I say it's my body and my right to smoke if I want to. It's not as though I'm hurting anyone else, after all.

    Faulty thinking/misinformation: _____

    _____

    Realities: _____

    _____

    _____

    _____

Quitters *Always* Win

Directions ➤ Choosing to become tobacco-free affords numerous health benefits to tobacco users. Yet, many smokers and other tobacco users choose not to quit, often because of a lack of information about the realities of quitting. The following is a list of misconceptions about kicking the habit, with accompanying facts. Present the misconceptions to at least five smokers and five nonsmokers in the form of either a survey or a true-or-false test. After administering the survey or test, share the truth about each statement. Use the space at the bottom of the page to record the individuals' reactions to learning the truth.

Misconception

1. It takes years for the benefits of quitting to show up.

2. The only true way to quit is "cold turkey," which can be difficult.

3. Nicotine gum and other substitutes have the opposite effect from the one intended. their addiction to nicotine.

4. Everyone who quits becomes fat because they substitute eating for smoking.

5. There is no such thing as quitting "for good"; everyone who tries to stop eventually lights up again.

6. Of all tobacco users, only cigarette smokers develop an addiction to nicotine.

Reality

1. In the first 24 hours, a smoker's heart rate slows and blood pressure drops.

2. Numerous techniques for quitting exist.

3. These products have been successful in helping tens of thousands of smokers break

4. Only a third of smokers gain weight; another third actually *lose* weight.

5. Each year approximately 1.3 million Americans kick the habit—permanently.

6. The nicotine in pipe tobacco, cigars, and smokeless tobacco products can be addictive.

Reactions:

CHAPTER 24 Study Guide

STUDY TIPS
- Read the Health Concepts for each lesson.
- Look up the meanings of any Health Terms that are unfamiliar.
- Read the questions below before you read the chapter.

Directions ➤ As you read the chapter, answer the following questions. Later you can use this guide to review the information in the chapter.

LESSON 1

1. Give three reasons why many teens start smoking.

_____

_____

_____

_____

2. What is an addiction?

_____

_____

3. What is a stimulant? Name a stimulant found in tobacco smoke.

_____

_____

4. Describe the effects on the body of the tar found in cigarettes.

_____

_____

5. What colorless, odorless, poisonous gas is passed into the lungs when a person smokes a cigarette?

_____

6. Name two other tobacco products besides cigarettes.

_____

LESSON 2

7. Name three diseases of the respiratory system associated with cigarette smoking.

_____

8. Name three ways in which cigarette smoking affects the circulatory system.

_____

_____

_____

9. Define *leukoplakia*.

_____

_____

10. Define each of the following kinds of passive smoke.

    a) Mainstream smoke: _____

    b) Sidestream smoke: _____

11. List three problems that smoking during pregnancy can cause to children before and after birth.

_____

_____

_____

LESSON 3

12. Name two symptoms a person might experience during nicotine withdrawal.

_____

_____

13. How do nicotine substitutes help a person stop smoking?

_____

_____

_____

14. Identify three steps a person can take to help him or her quit using tobacco.

_____

_____

_____

15. Name three physical benefits of giving up smoking.

_____

_____

_____

CHAPTER 25 Vocabulary

ethanol	designated drivers	binge drinking
fermentation	fatty liver	alcohol poisoning
intoxication	cirrhosis	alcoholism
blood alcohol concentration	fetal alcohol syndrome	delirium tremens (DTs)

Directions ➤ Read the following passage. For each underlined phrase, write the term from the list above that can replace it.

(1) The type of alcohol found in alcoholic beverages is a powerful drug. It is produced by (2) the chemical action of yeast on sugars. At some point in the consumption of alcohol, a state of (3) physical and mental impairment resulting from the use of alcohol sets in. Consumption of alcohol may lead to (4) a physical and psychological dependence on the drug ethanol. Children born to women who drank heavily during pregnancy may be affected by (5) a condition in which a fetus has been adversely affected mentally and physically.

(6) Periodic excessive drinking can lead to serious difficulties. When a person drinks a large amount of alcohol in a short period of time, he or she may experience (7) a dangerous toxic condition. Death can result when (8) the amount of alcohol in a person's blood reaches 400 mg per deciliter. Long-term alcohol abuse can result in (9) a condition in which fats build up in the liver and cannot be broken down and (10) a condition in which liver tissue is destroyed and replaced with scar tissue. When an alcoholic stops drinking, he or she might experience (11) the dramatic physical and psychological effects of alcohol withdrawal, which can include tremors, nightmares, and hallucinations.

1. _____

2. _____

3. _____

4. _____

5. _____

6. _____

7. _____

8. _____

9. _____

10. _____

11. _____

ACTIVITY **74** Applying Health Skills

Here's Looking Through You!

Directions ➤ As noted in the lesson, alcohol manufacturers spend over $1 billion a year advertising their product. Many of these ads use deceptive techniques or send hidden messages to make the products seem attractive—and harmless. Below is a typical ad. Examine the words and images it contains. Then answer the questions that follow.

1. How would you describe the mood of the ad? What images help convey this mood?

_____

_____

2. What words and phrases has the advertiser used to entice its audience into buying this product?

_____

_____

3. What facts about alcohol use is the ad deliberately omitting?

_____

_____

_____

ACTIVITY 75 Applying Health Skills

Witness for the Prosecution

Directions ➤ Below is a partial transcript from a court case involving a fatal traffic accident. The defendant, Frederick Snell, claims that his car's brakes failed, causing him to strike and kill a pedestrian. The prosecution is attempting to prove the defendant was DWI. In the section of the transcript shown, the defendant has taken the stand in his own defense. Help the prosecution make its case. In the box provided, indicate line numbers from Snell's testimony, along with facts from the lesson, that prove Dr. Snell is guilty as charged.

(1) **Defense Attorney:** Now, Dr. Snell, you contend that you
(2) were not drunk, although you do admit to having been
(3) drinking prior to getting behind the wheel of your car. How
(4) can you be sure that you were in fact sober, as you state?
(5) **Snell:** It's simple. First, as the police report confirms,
(6) my blood alcohol concentration was a mere 0.03 at the time
(7) of the accident—far beneath the intoxication threshold.
(8) Second, I had consumed only a single glass of bourbon. I
(9) couldn't *possibly* have been drunk from that!
(10) **Defense Attorney:** Thank you. By the way, Dr. Snell, would
(11) you mind telling the court what kind of doctor you are?
(12) **Snell:** Not at all—I'm a physician.
(13) **Defense Attorney:** Splendid. Then maybe you can explain
(14) to the court how long it takes an alcoholic beverage to affect
(15) a person's judgment following consumption.
(16) **Snell:** Certainly. It takes at least an hour—which further
(17) clears me of any wrongdoing. Scarcely 15 minutes had
(18) elapsed between the time I left the bar and the moment
(19) when that poor child stepped suddenly in front of my car.
(20) Furthermore, I had consumed several large glasses of water
(21) as I was settling up my bar tab, speeding up the oxidation
(22) of the alcohol by my body's liver.
(23) **Defense Attorney:** Thank you, Dr. Snell. Now the
(24) prosecution has made much of the fact that witnesses in the
(25) bar testify to having seen you place some sort of pill on your
(26) tongue and swallow. As a doctor, do you see any cause for
(27) concern over such an action.
(28) **Snell:** None whatsoever! I did indeed take a pill—an
(29) aspirin to be exact. I had spent much of the previous night
(30) in surgery and was suffering from a headache.
(31) **Defense Attorney:** Thank you, Dr. Snell—I have nothing
(32) more. *[Turning to attorney for the prosecution.]* Your
(33) witness.

Proof of Frederick Snell's Guilt:

_____

_____

_____

_____

_____

_____

_____

_____

_____

_____

_____

_____

_____

_____

_____

_____

_____

_____

_____

_____

_____

_____

ACTIVITY 76 **Applying Health Skills**

Taking Stock

Directions ➤ As noted in the lesson, choosing to be alcohol-free is one of the most important decisions you will ever make. One way of helping yourself make the right choice is by taking stock of your strengths and weaknesses. The self-questionnaire below will help you do just that. Complete the questionnaire and keep it in your private health journal.

1. Some of my accomplishments in the last year include:

   _____

   _____

2. In 5 years, I picture myself:

   _____

   _____

3. In 15 years, I picture myself:

   _____

   _____

4. The following hobby or pastime has helped me relax at times when I have felt tense:

   _____

   _____

5. The following are three people I feel comfortable talking to when I have a problem:

   _____

   _____

6. The following are three ways of saying no to peers and others when the need arises:

   _____

   _____

7. My most important reason for avoiding alcohol is:

   _____

   _____

CHAPTER 25 Study Guide

STUDY TIPS
- Read the Health Concepts for each lesson.
- Look up the meanings of any Health Terms that are unfamiliar.
- Read the questions below before you read the chapter.

Directions ➤ As you read the chapter, answer the following questions. Later you can use this guide to review the information in the chapter.

LESSON 1

1. What is ethanol?

_____

2. What are the two ways in which ethanol can be made?

_____

_____

3. What are three problems that alcohol use can cause for teens who engage in its use?

_____

_____

4. Give four reasons why young people drink.

_____

_____

_____

_____

5. Name three factors that affect teen alcohol use.

_____

LESSON 2

6. Briefly explain the short-term effects of alcohol on each of the following.

a) Brain: _____

_____

_____

b) Heart: _____

_____

c) Stomach: _____

_____

7. Define *blood alcohol concentration.*

_____

_____

8. Name three effects alcohol has on driving.

_____

_____

_____

_____

9. Define the following two chronic liver conditions that are the result of prolonged heavy alcohol use.

a) Fatty liver: _____

_____

b) Cirrhosis: _____

_____

10. Explain each of the following long-term effects of drinking.

a) Tolerance: _____

_____

b) Dependence: _____

_____

11. Define *fetal alcohol syndrome.*

_____

_____

LESSON 3

12. What is alcohol poisoning?

_____

_____

13. Identify three traits of a person inflicted with alcoholism.

_____

_____

_____

_____

14. During what stage of alcoholism might a drinker experience delirium tremens, or DTs? What are effects symptoms of DTs?

_____

_____

15. Name three costs of alcoholism to the family and to society.

_____

_____

CHAPTER 26 Vocabulary

substance abuse	paranoia	designer drugs
illegal drugs	euphoria	look-alike drugs
synthetic drugs	depressants	therapeutic
illicit drug use	narcotics	communities
gateway drugs	hallucinogens	Drug-Free School
overdose	marijuana	Zones
psychoactive drugs	hashish	drug watches
stimulants	inhalants	

Directions ➤ Etymology, the study of a word's origins, can provide clues to the meanings of an entire family of words and phrases. Using a dictionary that contains the etymology of words, investigate the origins of each word and phrase listed above. Then answer the questions that follow.

1. Which term in the list comes from both a Latin word meaning "to dream" and a Greek word meaning "to wander"?

   _____

2. Which term in the list descends from Greek roots meaning "faulty; abnormal" and "mind"?

   _____

3. Which term descends from a Greek root meaning "to breathe"? Name two words not from the list that share the same root.

   Term from list: _____

   Terms that share root: _____

4. Two terms that name illegal drugs are borrowed from other languages. Identify each term and the language from which it was borrowed.

   _____

5. Two terms in the list that are related in meaning are in part descended from Latin words with similar meanings. Identify the terms and their etymology. In what other way are the terms similar?

   _____

   _____

   _____

Risky Business

Directions ➤ As noted in the lesson, using drugs is a risky—and costly—business. Below are profiles of four users. Using information from the profiles and the lesson, match the user or users to each of the descriptions that follow.

A. Monique turned to alcohol when the daily shouting matches between her and her parents over school became too hard to take. In time she began experimenting with "harder" substances. This morning Monique found out that she is infected with HIV.

B. Burton's cocaine habit began at a party where he feared being ridiculed as the "odd man out" unless he tried it. That was four months ago, and now Burton needs more and more of the drug just to get high.

C. When Walanda and her husband found out last month that Walanda was pregnant, they decided that she should quit taking amphetamines. Recently, Walanda has begun having chills, extreme nausea, and headaches. Her husband thinks it is just a first sign of morning sickness.

D. Damon was feeling tense over tryouts for the school hockey team. When a marijuana cigarette was offered to him, he decided to try it in order to calm down and focus on his efforts. In time, he moved on to crack, and now he can't get through the day without a fix.

User(s)	Description
1. _____	Has developed a tolerance to a drug.
2. _____	May have taken drugs by means of injection.
3. _____	Began using drugs to escape problems.
4. _____	Began using drugs to relax.
5. _____	Is experiencing withdrawal.
6. _____	Has used a gateway drug.
7. _____	Began using drugs when felt pressured to do so and didn't know how to say no.
8. _____	Is showing symptoms of psychological dependence.
9. _____	May someday be the parent of a child with a drug dependency problem.

ACTIVITY 78 **Applying Health Skills**

At the Front Gate

Directions ➤ Ridgefield is a community that—unfortunately, like so many others across the country—has a drug problem. Below are "come-ons" from drug pushers that have been overheard near the front gate of Ridgefield High. Each contains deadly misinformation. Using the facts presented in the lesson, correct the information in each.

1. Psst, kid: I got some LSD here that will make you feel like you're on top of the world. The stuff is safe. It's out of your system within 24 hours.

   Corrected information: _____

   _____

   _____

   _____

   _____

2. If you want some cheap—and harmless—thrills, I can score some cough medicine with codeine for you. All you need is a swig, and you'll be feeling mellow. The best part is that this stuff is prescribed by doctors—so you know it has to be safe!

   Corrected information: _____

   _____

   _____

   _____

   _____

3. So, you got problems at home. Well, I've got something that will help you escape. It's called crack. There's no dirty needle with this drug, no pills to stay in your system a long time. This drug you smoke. Best of all, you can't get hooked on it. When you decide you've had enough, you just stop.

   Corrected information: _____

   _____

   _____

   _____

   _____

ACTIVITY 79 **Applying Health Skills**

More from Ridgefield High

Directions ➤ Below are more "come-ons" from drug pushers that have been overheard near the front gate of Ridgefield High. Each contains deadly misinformation. Using the facts presented in the lesson, correct the information in each.

1. Interested in making the football team—the easy way? These steroids are your answer. There are no side effects. You just take them and get bigger and stronger; it's as easy as that. Don't worry about anyone finding out, either. They're strictly legal. You have my word.

   Corrected information: _____

   _____

   _____

   _____

   _____

2. You know the problem with most drugs? They're illegal. That's why I sell only ecstasy. This drug contains absolutely no illegal substances, and, true to its name, it will put you in a state of ecstasy. It's the perfect pick-me-up for those times when you're feeling bored and need a little lift. Let me set you up with some.

   Corrected information: _____

   _____

   _____

   _____

   _____

3. You've heard all about how bad cigarettes are for you, haven't you? They cause lung cancer and other health problems. Not marijuana! Think of it as a worry-free cigarette. Plus, it does something cigarettes can't. It helps you feel loose and relaxed when your nerves are on edge.

   Corrected information: _____

   _____

   _____

   _____

   _____

ACTIVITY **80** Applying Health Skills

Ounce of Prevention

Directions ➤ As noted earlier in the chapter, drug use among 12 to 17-year-olds more than doubled during the decade of the 1990s. Some of these new users may be young people in your own community. If the drug use epidemic is to be stopped, it will require a widespread effort. You can do your part by completing the checklist that follows and posting it in a location where it is likely to be seen by many teens.

Drug Prevention Checklist

✓ Free and low-cost places to have healthful fun in this community:

Name: _____   Name: _____

Type of establishment: _____   Type of establishment: _____

_____   _____

Address: _____   Address: _____

Phone: _____   Phone: _____

Hours: _____   Hours: _____

✓ Community issues in which teen volunteers can become involved:

_____

✓ Community and national resources for teens and others with drug problems:

Help Line(s): _____

Residential treatment center(s): _____

✓ Useful phone numbers:

Cocaine Anonymous _____

Marijuana Anonymous _____

Narcotics Anonymous _____

Alcoholics Anonymous _____

✓ Drug watch headquarters in this community:

Address: _____

Phone: _____

Contact: _____

CHAPTER 27 Vocabulary

intervention	inpatient treatment	enabling
recovery	outpatient treatment	Al Anon
detoxification	halfway houses	detachment
relapses	codependents	Alateen

Directions ➤ Use the clues to solve the puzzle. Write one letter of each answer in the space provided. Copy the boxed letters in order to the spaces at the bottom of the page to spell out ways in which recovering addicts may be helped.

1. Learning to live an alcohol-free or drug-free life

2. Continuing care facilities for people recovering from addiction

3. People who become overly concerned with another's addiction problem

4. The process of pulling back or separating from involvement with someone else's addiction

5. A support program for people ages 12 to 20 whose parents, other family members, or friends have drinking problems

6. The removal of all drugs from the body

7. Trying to protect the person having trouble with alcohol or other drugs from facing the consequences of his or her drug-related problems

8. Slips from recovery

9. On-site medical and psychological care

10. Medical and psychological care during which a person stays at a medical or rehabilitation facility

11. A self-help organization for people who are close to alcoholics

12. Interruption of the addiction continuum before the addict or alcoholic hits bottom

1. ___ ___ ☐ ___ ___ ___ ___ ___

2. ___ ___ ___ ___ ___ ☐ ☐ ___ ___ ___ ___

3. ___ ___ ___ ___ ___ ☐ ___ ☐ ___

4. ___ ___ ___ ___ ☐ ___ ___ ___

5. ___ ☐ ___ ___ ___ ___ ___

6. ___ ___ ___ ___ ___ ☐ ___ ___ ___ ___ ☐ ___

7. ___ ___ ___ ___ ___ ___ ☐ ___ ___

8. ___ ___ ___ ☐ ___ ___ ___

9. ___ ☐ ___ ☐ ___ ___ ___ ___ ___ ___ ___ ___ ___ ___ ___ ___

10. ___ ___ ☐ ___ ___ ___ ___ ___ ___ ___ ___ ___ ___ ___

11. ___ ___ ___ - ___ ☐ ___ ___

12. ___ ___ ___ ___ ☐ ___ ___ ☐ ___ ___

Recovering alcoholics may be helped by _____ and _____.

ACTIVITY **81** Applying Health Skills

Your Call

Directions ➤ You are host of a radio talk show that deals in a frank manner with important topics. The topic for tonight's show is "Recovering from Addiction." Using information from the lesson, respond to each caller's questions and concerns.

Caller 1: "My friend says he doesn't need a detox unit—that when he's ready to quit drugs, he's going to go cold turkey and do it himself. Does he have the right idea?"

Your response: _____

_____

_____

_____

_____

Caller 2: "I used to have a drug problem, but I've been clean for two years. I've been going regularly to an outpatient treatment center, and I've stayed away from friends who I know use drugs. I think I'm recovered, but my counselor tells me I should still come for treatment. How can I explain to him that I'm over my addiction?"

Your response: _____

_____

_____

_____

_____

Caller 3: "My uncle was an alcoholic, and it was awful watching his life go down the drain. I swore nothing like that would ever happen to me. When I go out with my friends, I won't drink at all. My friend says I'm being ridiculous and that having just one drink is not going to make me an alcoholic. Are my friends right?"

Your response: _____

_____

_____

_____

_____

_____

ACTIVITY 82 **Applying Health Skills**

The Fall and Rise of the Smith Family

Directions ➤ A TV production company is preparing a fictional docudrama on a family suffering from a codependency problem. Unfortunately, the scenes have become misordered. Help the company get back on track. Reorder the scenes, which appear below, by copying the letter preceding each into the box provided. Then answer the questions that follow.

A. Scene ?: Mae Smith, with tears in her eyes, stands at the front door of her uncle's house; she tells her uncle tearfully that her mother has a problem.

B. Scene ?: Carl Smith sits in the office of a psychiatrist who specializes in chemical dependency.

C. Scene ?: Mae Smith, at her locker at school, overhears other students whispering that her mother has a drinking problem. Mae turns and screams that it is a lie.

D. Scene ?: Carl Smith stands at the stove preparing breakfast. He tells his two children, Mae and Alfie, that their mother is not feeling well, and that he will see them off to school this morning.

E. Scene ?: Carl Smith finally admits his involvement in his wife's addiction.

F. Scene ?: Mae and Alfie walk into the door where an Al-Anon meeting is taking place.

G. Scene ?: Carl Smith, his hair tousled and necktie askew, stands in Mae's room shouting that she had no right to air the family's dirty laundry with her uncle. She sits on her bed sobbing.

H. Scene ?: Carl, Mae, and Alfie appear at the home of friends, where they have been invited for dinner. Carl makes up an excuse that his wife Karen came down with a splitting headache at the last minute and couldn't attend.

Correct order of scenes: _____

1. Which member of the Smith family is an enabler? Explain your response.

_____

_____

2. Which family member takes the first step toward recovery? Describe the step taken.

_____

_____

3. What type of help does each of the Smith eventually seek?

_____

_____

CHAPTER 27 Study Guide

STUDY TIPS
- Read the Health Concepts for each lesson.
- Look up the meanings of any Health Terms that are unfamiliar.
- Read the questions below before you read the chapter.

Directions ➤ As you read the chapter, answer the following questions. Later you can use this guide to review the information in the chapter.

LESSON 1

1. Name three warning signs of possible addiction.

_____

_____

_____

_____

2. What is intervention?

_____

_____

3. Define *recovery*.

_____

4. What is the first step in the recovery process?

_____

5. Why do most experts recommend total abstinence from any mood-altering drugs for recovery?

_____

_____

_____

6. What are relapses?

_____

7. Name two different treatment options for a person with an addiction.

_____

8. What is the difference between inpatient treatment and outpatient treatment? In what way are the two similar?

_____

_____

_____

9. What are halfway houses?

_____

LESSON 2

10. Define *codependents*.

_____

_____

11. List three traits of codependents.

_____

_____

_____

_____

_____

12. What are enablers?

_____

_____

_____

13. What two steps must a codependent or an addicted family member take to get well?

_____

_____

14. Define *detachment*.

_____

_____

_____

15. Explain the difference between Al-Anon and Alateen.

_____

_____

_____

_____

CHAPTER 28 Vocabulary

infectious disease	phagocytosis	vaccine
parasites	neutrophils	immunization
virus	antibodies	rubella
transmission	pneumonia	active immunity
immunity	tuberculosis (TB)	passive immunity
mucous membranes	strep throat	

Directions ➤ Etymology, the study of a word's origins, can provide clues to the meanings of an entire family of words and phrases. Using a dictionary that contains the etymology of words, investigate the origins of each word and phrase listed above. Then answer the questions that follow.

1. Which term in the list comes from a Latin word meaning "venom, poisonous"?

   _____

2. Which term descends from two Latin roots meaning "across, beyond, through" and "to send"?

   _____

3. Which term in the list comes from a Latin word meaning "cow"? Explain why its origin is appropriate to its current meaning in English.

   _____

   _____

4. Which terms have the same root as the word *community* ("a unified body of individuals")? From what Latin word do these terms descend? What is its meaning?

   _____

   _____

5. Which term is descended from a Latin word that means "reddish"? Explain why its origin is appropriate to its meaning.

   _____

   _____

6. Identify the origin of each of the following terms. Explain why their origins are appropriate to their meanings.

   a) Pneumonia: _____

   _____

   b) Tuberculosis: _____

   _____

ACTIVITY 83 **Applying Health Skills**

In the Dark

Directions ➤ The Middle Ages—the period of European history from about A.D. 500 to 1500—is sometimes referred to as the *Dark Ages*. The bleak name derives from the cultural stagnation and lack of progress that typified the era. Widespread ignorance left the people open to a number of plagues, one of which—the Black Death—wiped out nearly three-quarters of the population. Below is a conversation that might have occurred among the elders of a village during one of those epidemics. Read the numbered paragraphs of the dialogue. Then, using information from the lesson, correct any factual errors on the corresponding numbered lines.

1. "My brothers, I believe I know what is causing this disease," declared Gandolfo. "It is a phantom that lurks in the shadows after sundown. "I suggest that we urge all townspeople to remain within their homes, barring the door by night."

2. "Yea, verily," added Randolfo. "We should, moreover, implore the good people to bring their animals inside their homes with them at night. Livestock is entitled to protection from the scourge!"

3. Pandolfo now spoke. "All I know is that in my home we share eating utensils only among family members. That way we will be protected."

4. "What of the town council suggestion that we stop burning the goods and clothes of those who have died?" said Gandolfo. "Some complain, and rightly, that these things are hard to come by. I submit that we order the families of the dead to thoroughly wipe off any possessions they touched."

5. Pandolfo snuffled. "The most important thing is to get the sickness out from the body. I recommend that we encourage the townspeople not to cover up when they cough or sneeze. Covering up only gives the sickness one road to travel: back inside the body."

6. Randolfo nodded in agreement. "We must also ensure that all townspeople air out their food before eating it. The rule at my home is to expose slaughtered meats to the air for at least five days. I think we should encourage all to do the same."

7. "Yes," said Gandolfo, "and we must also give the families of the sick special privileges. Since we are also amidst a drought, they alone should be permitted to refill their jugs with water from the town well."

1. _____

2. _____

_____

3. _____

4. _____

_____

5. _____

_____

_____

6. _____

_____

7. _____

ACTIVITY 84 **Applying Health Skills**

Making the Rounds

Directions ➤ You are assisting the doctors making rounds at a local hospital. Below are charts of patients on the ward. Review each patient's symptoms. Using that information along with information from the lesson, complete each chart.

County General Hospital

PATIENT #1

SYMPTOMS: *Patient reports having lost considerable weight in recent weeks, partly as a result of a diminished appetite, partly because the patient's persistent hacking cough makes eating difficult. Patient was brought to hospital based on belief he was having a heart attack—was experiencing chest pain, shortness of breath, fever, sweating.*

POSSIBLE DIAGNOSIS: _____

RECOMMENDED TREATMENT: _____

_____

_____

County General Hospital

PATIENT #2

SYMPTOMS: *Patient initially assumed she was having a bout with the flu—symptoms included fever and nausea accompanied by pain in her joints and aching muscles. The condition, however, failed to change after several weeks, causing some concern. Husband brought patient to hospital upon noticing a yellowish tinge to her skin and the whites of her eyes.*

POSSIBLE DIAGNOSIS: _____

RECOMMENDED TREATMENT: _____

_____

_____

County General Hospital

PATIENT #3

SYMPTOMS: *Patient, who is six years old, is running a fever. Entire body is covered with tiny red dots. Upon being confronted, parents admit to having been a little lax in keeping up with child's immunizations.*

POSSIBLE DIAGNOSIS: _____

POSSIBLE COMPLICATIONS: _____

_____

_____

County General Hospital

PATIENT #4

SYMPTOMS: *Male patient was rushed to hospital when symptoms that his wife perceived to be signs of a cold—headache and fever—escalated into more serious symptoms, including confusion and mild paralysis.*

POSSIBLE DIAGNOSIS: _____

OTHER SYMPTOMS THAT MAY APPEAR: _____

_____

_____

ACTIVITY 85   **Applying Health Skills**

Teen Vaccinations

Directions ➤ The American Medical Association's "Guidelines for Adolescent Preventive Services" recommends that all adolescents in this country be properly immunized. Specifically, they recommend the schedule below. Use the schedule to complete the checklist for yourself and for any adolescent brothers or sisters living in your home. Keep this checklist with other important papers. Safeguard your health by referring to it from time to time.

Immunization Schedule

Vaccine	Administered . . .
bivalent TB booster	at ages 11 to 12 and every 10 years thereafter.
second dose of MMR	at ages 11 to 12 unless there exists proof of two vaccinations earlier in childhood.
Hepatitis B	at ages 11 to 12, or older if unvaccinated and take part in high-risk behaviors.
Hepatitis A	to teens traveling in countries with high or moderate incidence of hepatitis A virus.
varicella	at ages 11 to 12, if not immunized as part of a routine childhood schedule or known to be vaccinated against chickenpox.

Checklist

	Self	Teen Sibling(s)
■ Date of most recent vaccination (to be updated periodically; add lines as needed)	_____ _____ _____ _____	_____ _____ _____ _____
■ Diseases immunized against to date	a) _____ b) _____ c) _____ d) _____ e) _____	a) _____ b) _____ c) _____ d) _____ e) _____
■ Conditions in Teen Immunization schedule above that are relevant (e.g., traveling abroad)	a) _____ b) _____ c) _____	a) _____ b) _____ c) _____

CHAPTER 28 Study Guide

STUDY TIPS
- Read the Health Concepts for each lesson.
- Look up the meanings of any Health Terms that are unfamiliar.
- Read the questions below before you read the chapter.

Directions ➤ As you read the chapter, answer the following questions. Later you can use this guide to review the information in the chapter.

LESSON 1

1. What is an infectious disease?

_____

_____

2. Name three of the possible forms pathogens can take.

_____

3. Describe the makeup of viruses.

_____

_____

4. What are protozoans?

_____

5. Identify three ways in which infectious diseases are spread.

_____

_____

6. Identify the body's four nonspecific defenses against infection.

_____

_____

7. What are the two main types of lymphocytes involved in the body's specific response to infection?

_____

LESSON 2

8. Identify two respiratory infections and their symptoms.

_____

_____

_____

9. Tell what causes each of the following.

a) Meningitis: _____

b) Poliomyelitis: _____

ACTIVITY 86 **Applying Health Skills**

Myth-Information

Directions ➤ Below are snippets of dialogues—conversations between two people. Each snippet contains a statement revealing a myth or other piece of misinformation about STDs. For each entry, list the myth or misinformation and then present the facts.

1. *[Into telephone receiver.]* Anyway, Ciel, there I was at the mall with Rhondelle, and we both had to use the powder room. As it turns out, this awful, dirty woman used the same stall just before I did. I didn't know it at the time—Rhondelle told me later. Now I'm sure I have some sort of sexual disease! Ciel, I swear—that's the last time, ever, I use any toilet other than my own at home!

   Myth or misinformation: _____

   The facts: _____

   _____

   _____

2. *[Male talking to another in locker room.]* Man, am I relieved! You remember me telling you about those sores I had on my hands and feet? Well, they're gone—disappeared just like that. After getting that scary news from Marguerite a while back, I thought I might have the same STD she had. I'm just glad it cleared up all by itself.

   Myth or misinformation: _____

   The facts: _____

   _____

   _____

3. *[Young woman to friend.]* John's been pressuring me again to have sex with him. I told him that with all I had heard about sexual diseases, I didn't know if I was ready to deal with any of it. John said if I was really worried, he'd take me to a clinic he knows to get a vaccination against them.

   Myth or misinformation: _____

   The facts: _____

   _____

   _____

ACTIVITY 87 **Applying Health Skills**

More Myth-Information

Directions ➤ Below are more snippets of dialogues—conversations between two people. Each snippet contains a statement revealing a myth or other piece of misinformation about STDs. For each entry, list the myth or misinformation and then present the facts.

1. *[Into telephone receiver.]* I don't know what I'm going to do, Kelly. I think I have gonorrhea. I can't tell my mother or father. I'm so afraid. I know I'm going to die from this disease. I read someplace that there's no cure for it!

   Myth or misinformation: _____

   The facts: _____

   _____

   _____

2. *[Young female at desk writing letter to cousin.]* My boyfriend has the ugliest cold sore I've ever seen. He told me it was nothing to worry about—that, even though it's herpes, it's not the genital kind. Besides, he said, even if it were genital herpes, it wouldn't be contagious once the blister appears.

   Myth or misinformation: _____

   The facts: _____

   _____

   _____

3. *[Man to doctor as he buttons up shirt at the end of routine checkup.]* Oh, one other thing I forgot to mention: I had this weird rash on my chest last week. It didn't even itch or anything. I thought maybe I had some new kind of measles. Oh, yeah—and about a month before that, I had this sore but it didn't hurt. I have nothing to worry about, right?

   Myth or misinformation: _____

   The facts: _____

   _____

   _____

CHAPTER 30 **Vocabulary**

| acquired immune deficiency syndrome (AIDS) | intravenous (IV) drugs | confirmatory test |
| human immunodefi- ciency virus (HIV) | HIV-reactive ELISA (EIA) | latency AIDS-opportunistic illnesses (AIDS-OIs) |

Directions ➤ A number of different relationships exist among words and phrases and the ideas they represent.

- A *hierarchical relationship* is a relationship in which one word is higher in rank than another. Examples: *boss → employee; teacher → student.*
- A *cause-effect relationship* is a relationship in which a condition or event represented by one word is a possible cause of a condition or event represented by another. Examples: *rain → wet; accident → injury.*
- A *parallel relationship* is a relationship in which two or more words share an equivalent status. Examples: *brother → sister; apple → orange.*

Use the information on word relationships to answer the questions that follow.

1. What type of relationship exists among the terms *HIV, AIDS,* and *IV drugs*? In which order should these terms logically appear?

   _____

2. What type of relationship exists between the terms *ELISA (EIA)* and *confirmatory test*? Explain your answer. What type of relationship exists between those terms and the term *HIV-reactive*?

   _____

   _____

   _____

   _____

3. To which term in the above list would *MAI, PCP,* and *CMV* stand in a hierarchical relationship? Explain that relationship.

   _____

   _____

ACTIVITY 88 **Applying Health Skills**

Mixed Messages

Directions ➤ Imagine that you were helping a friend create an outline for a report on HIV/AIDS. Your friend has clipped bits of information from a number of different sources, some reliable and some not. Read the headlines, which appear below. Help organize the information for the report. First, draw a line through headlines based on misunderstanding. Then, arrange those that are accurate in an outline, adding facts from the lesson as needed.

Man Gets HIV from Toilet

Human Health and Services Secretary: Abstinence Is the Key to Preventing HIV

Teenage HIV Infection on the Rise

Mother Gives Birth to AIDS Babies

Woman Sues Tattoo Parlor; Claims "I Got HIV from One of Their Dirty Needles!"

Study Links Contaminated Needles and HIV

Study Shows that "Bad" Blood from Transfusions Is Main Way of Contracting HIV

Health Club Ejects Member Found to Be HIV-Reactive

Dancing Linked to Spread of AIDS

New Scientific Findings Show AIDS Virus Fools Immune System

Small Concentrations of HIV Found in Breast Milk

Researchers Discover Link Between Lymphocytes and Antibodies

Outline:

_____

_____

_____

_____

_____

_____

_____

_____

_____

_____

_____

_____

_____

_____

ACTIVITY 89 **Applying Health Skills**

A Little Learning

Directions ➤ The World Health Organization estimates that the number of cases of HIV infection will reach 40 million within the next few years. The key to altering such grim statistics is HIV/AIDS education. The table below, compiled by the Centers for Disease Control and Prevention, shows the effects of a nationwide effort to educate high school students about HIV/AIDS. Using the information in the table, answer the questions that follow.

Grade	Percent Taught about HIV/AIDS Infection in School	Percent Who Talked with Parents or Adult Family Member about HIV/AIDS
9	86.0	58.9
10	87.8	65.0
11	84.8	65.2
12	86.8	63.7

Source: CDC Youth Risk Behavior Survey, 1995

1. Would you consider the education effort in this country to be a success to date? Explain your response.

_____

_____

_____

2. Why do you think the individuals conducting the survey were interested in the numbers of respondents who had spoken with adult family members about HIV/AIDS?

_____

_____

3. Determine how students in your school measure up to national standards by conducting a survey of your own. Use the form below.

	Number of Students Polled	Percent Taught about HIV/AIDS Infection in School	Percent Who Talked with Parents or Adult Family Member about HIV/AIDS
9th-graders			
10th-graders			
11th-graders			
12th-graders			

CHAPTER **30** Study Guide

STUDY TIPS
- Read the Health Concepts for each lesson.
- Look up the meanings of any Health Terms that are unfamiliar.
- Read the questions below before you read the chapter.

Directions ➤ As you read the chapter, answer the following questions. Later you can use this guide to review the information in the chapter.

LESSON 1

1. What is the difference between HIV and AIDS?

_____

_____

2. Name three bodily fluids through which HIV is known to be transmitted.

_____

_____

3. Name the two most common means through which people become infected with HIV.

_____

_____

4. Define *intravenous drugs*.

_____

5. Explain how an unborn child can become infected with HIV.

_____

_____

LESSON 2

6. What is the term used to describe a person who is infected with HIV?

_____

7. What is ELISA?

_____

_____

8. Why is a confirmatory test sometimes used to diagnose HIV?

_____

_____

9. Define *latency*, and tell what the average latency period is before person shows indications of HIV infection.

_____

_____

10. What does AIDS-OIs stand for? What are AIDS-OIs?

_____

_____

_____

11. Briefly explain each of the following AIDS-OIs.

a) Pneumocystis carinii pneumonia: _____

_____

b) Toxoplasmosis gondii: _____

_____

c) Peripheral nerve/spinal cord dysfunction: _____

_____

12. Why have researchers geared their treatment efforts toward attacking the virus as soon as possible after the initial infection?

_____

_____

_____

13. Give two reasons why HIV and AIDS are difficult to research and treat.

_____

_____

_____

14. How is a pandemic different from an epidemic?

_____

_____

15. What is the best way to avoid getting HIV and AIDS?

_____

_____

CHAPTER **31** Vocabulary

noninfectious diseases	cancers	impaired glucose tolerance (IGT)
cardiovascular diseases (CVDs)	tumors	arthritis
	benign	rheumatoid arthritis
	malignant	osteoarthritis
hypertension	metastasis	disability
arteriosclerosis	carcinogen	profound deafness
angina pectoris	melanoma	mental retardation
fibrillation	biopsy	Americans with Disabilities Act
congestive heart failure	chemotherapy	
stroke	diabetes	
	insulin	

Directions ➤ Many of the words in the list above are related in some way. Create categories for as many words as possible. Then develop a heading for each category that illustrates how the words are related. For example, *rheumatoid arthritis* and *osteoarthritis* might be grouped with other terms under the heading "Types of Arthritis." Add your headings to the chart below. Then write words from the list under the appropriate headings.

			Types of Arthritis	
			rheumatoid arthritis osteoarthritis	

ACTIVITY 90 Applying Health Skills

Back on the Ward

Directions ➤ Read the patients' charts below. All the patients suffer from cardiovascular disease. Using that information along with information in the lesson, complete each chart.

Patient 1: male, white, age 68

Symptoms and Other Relevant Information: When the patient failed to answer his wife's call to breakfast this morning, she went to investigate and found the patient lying on the bedroom floor. The patient, who was conscious, told his wife that prior to his fall, he had experienced a sudden numbness on one side of his body and that his vision was cloudy. The patient has a history of hypertension. He is experiencing some difficulties with speech and seems to that have trouble understanding what others say to him. A further examination revealed a restricted blood flow to the heart due to a clogged artery.

Risk Factors for CVD: _____

Possible Diagnosis: _____

_____

Recommended Treatment: _____

_____

Patient 2: female, African American, age 44

Symptoms and Other Relevant Information: The patient was brought into the hospital after complaining of a pain in her chest that extended down her right arm. She was also experiencing shortness of breath and nausea. The patient has a family history of hypertension. A routine intake examination revealed that the patient is 30 pounds overweight.

Risk Factors for CVD: _____

Possible Diagnosis: _____

_____

Recommended Behavioral Changes: _____

_____

Patient 3: male, Asian, age 57

Symptoms and Other Relevant Information: After a typical lunch of two cheeseburgers, a milk-shake, and pie, the patient claims to have experienced a sharp pain in the chest that lasted only a few minutes. He has experienced similar pain in the past, sometimes not related to eating. The patient came to the hospital on his own power to confirm his own diagnosis of heartburn. The patient's weight is in the normal range.

Risk Factors for CVD: _____

Possible Diagnosis: _____

_____

Recommended Treatment and Behavioral Changes: _____

_____

ACTIVITY 91 Applying Health Skills

Haves and Have-Nots

Directions ➤ The good news is that more and more people are learning about behaviors that can decrease the risk of cancer. The bad news is that not everyone is acting on this information. Below are profiles of several typical Americans. Each has adopted certain positive habits in recent years but, at the same time, has maintained or acquired habits that increase his or her cancer risks. Beneath each profile is a pair of boxes labeled "Has" and "Has Not." In the "Has" box, list steps the person has taken to reduce cancer risks. In the "Has Not" box, list actions the person has not taken but *should* take. The first profile has been partly completed for you.

1. Last year, Consuela's New Year's resolutions included getting more exercise and eating more healthfully. True to her word, she has a large glass of orange juice each morning with a half pound of bacon and bicycles one hour every day. As a bonus for her hard work, she is even developing a deep, golden tan.

Has	Has Not
become physically active	reduced the amount of animal fats in the foods she eats

2. Gil has switched to a brand of cigarettes lower in tar and drinks only "light" beer when out partying with his buddies. Since he is in his fifties, Gil has also started seeing his doctor for regular rectal exams and has memorized the seven warning signs of cancer.

Has	Has Not

3. Kathy has learned the proper technique for doing a breast self-exam. In the hope of losing some of the 40 extra pounds she has carried around for years, she has also begun swimming two laps in the community pool each day.

Has	Has Not

| **ACTIVITY 92** | **Applying Health Skills** | FOR USE WITH CHAPTER 31, LESSON 3 |

Addled Ads

Directions ➤ One of the most fertile markets for peddlers of unscrupulous products is the health area. Back pages of magazines and supermarket tabloids are filled with fantastic claims for products "guaranteed to cure" almost any ailment, from chicken pox to cancer. Below are two misguided ads for noninfectious diseases covered in the lesson. Read each ad. Then identify the myths and misconceptions.

Good news for the over 1 million Americans suffering from type 1 and type 2 diabetes!

Nature's Miracle® proudly presents Dia-Beat-It, a revolutionary cure for this dreaded disease. No need for costly glucose shots, boring exercise, or tedious diets. Just pop one Dia-Beat-It tablet in your mouth each morning, and you're set for the day! Eat what you want. . . when you want it. All natural, too!

Myths and Misconceptions: _____

_____

_____

_____

"My muscles have stopped aching—*completely*!"

Testimonials like this are common. . . at least, among arthritic patients who have tried Arthrigon, the new arthritis remedy from the laboratories at Nature's Miracle®. Arthrigon is a secret blend of tree barks and spices guaranteed to kill the virus that causes this "old people's disease." Arthrigon works on both rheumatoid arthritis and the more deadly osteoarthritis by sending natural rays of heat to muscle centers, thereby renewing them. Throw away your heating pad, your antibiotics, and even your doctor's phone number! With Arthrigon, you'll feel great in no time!

Myths and Misconceptions: _____

_____

_____

_____

ACTIVITY 93 Applying Health Skills

Community Report Card

Directions ➤ More and more communities are taking steps to accommodate their physically challenged residents by providing wider doorways and ramps for enhanced wheelchair access and telephones equipped with sound-amplification devices (TTDs). The checklist below will give you an opportunity to learn how your community stacks up in these areas. Conduct a walking tour of your school and the other facilities listed, adding still others, if necessary. For each facility visited, assign a letter grade—A through F—and jot down any comments that seem appropriate. You may want to share your report card with community officials.

Checklist

■ School

Name: _____

Address: _____

Grade: _____

Comments: _____

■ Store or Other Retail Establishment

Name: _____

Address: _____

Grade: _____

Comments: _____

■ Library

Address: _____

Grade: _____

Comments: _____

■ Playground

Address: _____

Grade: _____

Comments: _____

■ Park

Address: _____

Grade: _____

Comments: _____

■ Mall

Address: _____

Grade: _____

Comments: _____

■ Other

Name: _____

Address: _____

Grade: _____

Comments: _____

CHAPTER **31** Study Guide

STUDY TIPS
- Read the Health Concepts for each lesson.
- Look up the meanings of any Health Terms that are unfamiliar.
- Read the questions below before you read the chapter.

Directions ➤ As you read the chapter, answer the following questions. Later you can use this guide to review the information in the chapter.

LESSON 1

1. What are cardiovascular diseases?

_____

2. Identify four risk factors that can increase a person's chance of developing a CVD.

_____

3. Why is hypertension known as the "silent killer"?

_____

_____

4. What is *atherosclerosis*?

_____

_____

_____

5. Name four procedures used to detect or treat heart disease by measuring the heart's electrical activity.

_____

_____

_____

6. Give three ways in which cardiovascular disease can be prevented.

_____

_____

_____

LESSON 2

7. Explain the relationship between tumors and cancers.

_____

_____

8. What is the term for a cancer-causing substance in the environment?

_____

9. What is the single greatest cause of lung cancer in the United States today?

_____

10. Define each of the following procedures related to the detection or treatment of cancer.

    a) Biopsy: _____

    _____

    b) Chemotherapy: _____

    _____

LESSON 3

11. Define *diabetes*.

_____

_____

12. Briefly explain each of the following types of diabetes.

    a) Type 1 diabetes: _____

    _____

    b) Type 2 diabetes: _____

    _____

13. Define each of the following kinds of arthritis.

    a) Rheumatoid arthritis: _____

    _____

    b) Osteoarthritis: _____

    _____

LESSON 4

14. What is a disability?

_____

_____

15. What is the purpose of the Americans with Disabilities Act?

_____

_____

_____

CHAPTER 32 Vocabulary

health care	health insurance	medical history
providers	Medicare	generic
primary care	Medicaid	quackery
physician	health maintenance	advocate
specialist	organization (HMO)	public health
health care facility	preferred provider	epidemiology
outpatient surgical	organization (PPO)	famine
facility	health consumer	

Directions ➤ A number of different relationships exist among words and phrases and the ideas they represent.

- A *hierarchical relationship* is a relationship in which one word is higher in rank than another. Examples: *supervisor → trainee, medium → small.*
- A *cause-effect relationship* is a relationship in which a condition or event represented by one word is a possible cause of a condition or event represented by another. Examples: *infection → fever, fatigue → sleep.*
- A *parallel relationship* is a relationship in which two or more words share an equivalent status. Examples: *girl → boy, elm → oak.*

Use the information on word relationships to answer the questions that follow.

1. Write a sentence that explains the parallel relationship between the terms *primary care physician* and *specialist.*

   _____

   _____

2. Identify two terms from the list that have a cause-effect relationship with the term *public health.* Explain that relationship.

   _____

   _____

   _____

   _____

3. What type of relationship exists among the terms *Medicare, Medicaid,* and *preferred provider organization?*

   _____

   _____

4. Identify a term from the list that has a hierarchical relationship with the term *health consumer.* Explain that relationship.

   _____

   _____

ACTIVITY 94 Applying Health Skills

Help Wanted

Directions ➤ Below are classified ads from the help-wanted section of a professional health journal. For each ad, write the job title of the professional being sought and whether
the opening is for a physician, a nurse, or an allied medical professional. The first
ad has been partly completed for you.

1. Wanted for part-time position at large city medical complex. Responsibilities will include patient
care and supervision of staff of LPNs. Leadership qualities a must. Send résumé to Box A793 c/o
this journal.

    Type of professional: _____

    Area of opening: Nurse.

2. Candidate for this hospital staff position will have had minimum of eight years treating patients
with various types of malignancies. Send résumé to Box A884 c/o this journal.

    Type of professional: _____

    Area of opening: _____

3. Needed: Suburban dentist's office seeks professional with minimum five years experience cleaning
and polishing teeth. College degree a plus. Send résumé to Box A197 c/o this journal.

    Type of professional: _____

    Area of opening: _____

4. The Old Orchard Nursing Home has an opening for an individual who can plan menus for patients
with varying needs and health requirements. Will offer nutritional counseling to patients and their
family members. Send résumé to Box A653 c/o this journal.

    Type of professional: _____

    Area of opening: _____

5. Private practice offering primary health care to children in Gifford County area seeks partner.
Degree from a local medical school is preferable. Qualified individuals should send their résumé to
Box A201 c/o this journal.

    Type of professional: _____

    Area of opening: _____

6. Rehabilitation hospital seeks professional with advanced degree in nursing to assist with patient
load. Will function essentially as primary care physician. Salary negotiable. If interested, contact:
Box A376 c/o this journal.

    Type of professional: _____

    Area of opening: _____

ACTIVITY 95 **Applying Health Skills**

On to Plan B

Directions ➤ Below are brochures for two different health plans. Compare the claims and features of each. Using this information, help the prospective health consumers choose a plan that is best for them.

Larkin Health Plan, Inc.

Albion County's Largest Health Maintenance Organization

Larkin's 35 physician members can provide all the care you need at affordable prices.

Some commonly asked questions:

Q. Who is eligible?
A. All residents of Albion County and their families.
Q. How much will coverage cost?
A. Larkin charges a fee of $50 per plan subscriber. After that, any visit to any plan doctor costs you only $15, and all prescription medicines cost $5. Hospital stays are reimbursed at 50 percent of all charges incurred.
Q. What charges are covered?
A. All office visits to plan physicians, all prescription medicines, all hospital stays. Exceptions: Larkin does not cover dental work, emergency room charges, or psychotherapy.

The National American Insurance Companies

(NAIC) proudly offers health insurance to all Americans under age 60. The country's foremost insurer offers this special plan at an introductory rate of $200 per year per new subscriber.* No plan doctors or waiting periods. Visit the doctor of your choice every time!

How NAIC Works

It's simple. Visit your doctor as you've always done. NAIC will reimburse your visits at 80 percent and prescription medicine costs at 70 percent.

Need surgery? No problem. As a member of the NAIC family, all hospital stays and emergency room visits are covered at 50%. We even pay for a portion of your dental checkups! Few plans can make that offer.

* Charge is assessed for each family member up to three members. Subject to increases to market rates after first anniversary in plan.

Prospective Health Consumers:

1. John and Rita Wicklowe's son Kevin is an asthmatic. He was rushed to the emergency room three times last year at a cost of $150 per visit. If the Wicklowes were going to choose a plan based on that fact alone, which plan would you recommend? Explain your reasoning.

_____

2. What other factors might the Wicklowe's need to consider in making their decision?

_____

_____

_____

3. George Latham just turned 57 and faces mandatory retirement in five years. What details of the NAIC plan should he pay careful attention to before choosing it?

_____

_____

_____

4. Mara Vanderbilt regularly takes a prescription medicine that costs $65. Assuming that she satisfies eligibility requirements for both plans, which plan should she choose?

_____

ACTIVITY 96 **Applying Health Skills**

Complaint Department

Directions ➤ You have taken a job with a consumer advocacy group in your community. Below are some of the complaint letters that have come in this week. Using information from the lesson, tell each letter writer what action he or she should take.

Letter 1: I went to a skin doctor for this rash on my arm. He gave me a prescription for an ointment, which I had filled at my local pharmacy. After using the ointment as directed for a week, I noticed that the rash was getting worse. When I called the doctor, he told me that my beef was with the pharmacy, not him—then he hung up the phone. I've since been to the pharmacy, but the pharmacist contends he was simply following the doctor's orders and that his hands are tied. I feel as though I am caught in the middle.

Your reply: _____

_____

_____

_____

_____

Letter 2: I saw this magazine ad for a product called *Pounds Off* that is supposed to help you lose weight while eating all your favorite foods. I sent away for the pills and tried them for a month, during which time I gained 14 pounds. The manufacturer won't return my phone calls or letters.

Your reply: _____

_____

_____

_____

_____

Letter 3: I bought a mail-order product I saw advertised on TV. It was supposed to take away wrinkles and make you look younger. I have since had two skin graft operations to cover burns on my face left by this horrible product! The stuff is no longer advertised, and letters I have sent to the address on the package have come back to me marked "Return to Sender." My face will never be the same. How can I get even?

Your reply: _____

_____

_____

_____

_____

ACTIVITY 97 **Applying Health Skills**

Seeing Red

Directions ➤ Among the organizations mentioned in the lesson that attend to public health issues on the global level is the International Red Cross. Begun as an agency to assist wounded soldiers, the Red Cross has since expanded its mission at both the international and community levels. The passage below provides some background on this important public health organization. Read the passage. Then answer the questions that follow.

The Red Cross was started in Switzerland during the nineteenth century. Today, the organization, which is headquartered in Geneva, Switzerland, has chapters and affiliates in 160 nations. Among these affiliates are the Red Crescent and the Red Star of David, the names by which the Red Cross is known, respectively, in Muslim countries and in Israel.

Whenever a disaster occurs—whether it is a war or a natural disaster such as an earthquake, a flood, or a fire—the Red Cross steps in. The agency provides medical treatment as well as food, clothing, and shelter. In addition, the Red Cross facilitates communication and provides counseling and financial assistance to those in need.

In recent decades, the Red Cross has also begun to sponsor classes in such areas as first aid, water safety, cardiopulmonary resuscitation (CPR), home nursing, and preparation for parenthood. You may associate the Red Cross with its blood donation efforts. The agency collects blood from volunteers, which is used for blood transfusions where needed.

1. Using an online or print resource, learn about another of the public health organizations mentioned in the lesson—the World Health Organization (WHO). Tell in what way WHO is similar to and different from the International Red Cross.

   _____

   _____

   _____

   _____

2. Contact a chapter of the American Red Cross in your own community to find out the following.

   a) Which of the specific classes mentioned in the passage are provided?

   _____

   b) What are the hours of the classes offered?

   _____

   c) Where are the classes held (for example, at the Red Cross, at a community swimming pool)?

   _____

   d) What is the outcome of taking a Red Cross course (for example, certification in a particular area or skill)?

   _____

   e) What other services mentioned in the passage are provided?

   _____

CHAPTER 32   Study Guide

STUDY TIPS
- Read the Health Concepts for each lesson.
- Look up the meanings of any Health Terms that are unfamiliar.
- Read the questions below before you read the chapter.

Directions ➤   As you read the chapter, answer the following questions. Later you can use this guide to review the information in the chapter.

LESSON 1

1. What is the term for the group of professionals trained in the health care field, from physicians to allied medical professionals?

   _____

2. Explain the difference between a primary care physician and a specialist.

   _____

   _____

   _____

3. Name four allied medical professionals.

   _____

   _____

   _____

4. Give two examples of each of the following.

   a) Short-term health care facility: _____

   _____

   b) Long-term health care facility: _____

   _____

5. Compare and contrast each of the following.

   a) Medicare and Medicaid: _____

   _____

   _____

   _____

   b) A health maintenance organization (HMO) and a preferred provider organization (PPO):

   _____

   _____

   _____

LESSON 2

6. Define *health consumer.*

   _____

7. What three factors need to be taken into account when choosing a health plan?

   _____

8. Give three guidelines to follow when choosing a health care provider.

   _____

   _____

   _____

9. List three qualities of a good patient.

   _____

   _____

10. What is a generic medicine?

    _____

LESSON 3

11. What is quackery?

    _____

12. Explain how each of the following agencies and organizations helps consumers with complaints against health care providers or products.

    a) Licensing board: _____

       _____

    b) Better Business Bureau: _____

       _____

13. What is an advocate?

    _____

LESSON 4

14. Define *public health.*

    _____

15. Name three agencies of the Department of Health and Human Services.

    _____

    _____

    _____

    _____

CHAPTER **33** **Vocabulary**

acid rain	particulates	deforestation
greenhouse effect	asbestos	desertification
chlorofluorocarbons (CFCs)	biodegradable	conservation
	hazardous wastes	recycling

Directions ➤ Analyzing the parts that make up a word can help you determine the meaning of the whole word. For example, if you know that one of the meanings of the prefix *in-* is "not" and are familiar with the word parts *ex-*, *plic-*, and *-able*, then you can determine that the word inexplicable means "unable to be explained." Using a good dictionary, analyze the parts of each word and phrase listed above. (Be aware of spelling changes when word parts are combined.) Then answer the questions that follow.

1. Give the meaning of each part of the following words and the meaning of the word as a whole.

a) Biodegradable: _____

_____

b) Desertification: _____

_____

c) Recycling: _____

_____

d) Hazardous: _____

_____

2. Several of the words in the list contain the suffix *-tion*. Explain how this suffix changed the words to which it was added.

_____

_____

3. Explain the difference between the letters *de-* at the beginning of the words *deforestation* and *desertification*.

_____

_____

4. Explain how the term *chlorofluorocarbons* was created.

_____

_____

_____

ACTIVITY 98 **Applying Health Skills**

Film at 11

Directions ➤ You are watching the evening news with your family. The people next door have put up a satellite dish, which is interfering with your family's TV reception. As a result, the sound and picture on your set are occasionally lost. Help your family keep up on world events by filling in probable missing information from the broadcast.

"Good evening, and welcome to *World News This Minute*. Today outside of Paris, violence erupted between protesters and management of Biochême Corporation. Biochême, a leading international manufacturer of chlorofluorocarbons, sells its product to half a dozen industries, including . . ." *[TV reception is lost.]*

1. Missing information: _____

_____

_____

[Reception is restored.] "Closer to home, the debate among city officials over the projected opening next month of a rebuilt blast furnace in Denton's Grove rages on. The anti-furnace faction has claimed that the furnace will put out great quantities of toxins, including lead. World News This Minute's Jerry Tyler is on hand to assess the possible health problems . . ." *[TV reception is lost.]*

2. Missing information: _____

_____

_____

[Reception is restored.] "Thank you, Jerry Tyler. Now this just in: An oil tanker off the coast of Alaska has spilled 150,000 gallons of crude oil into the Bering Strait. Experts and work crews have already helicoptered to the site. We switch you to KPDQ science editor Whit Blakemore, who is standing by in Nome to explain the long-term ramifications of this type of spill . . . ." *[TV reception is lost.]*

3. Missing information: _____

_____

_____

_____

ACTIVITY 99 Applying Health Skills

Panzozo's Problem

Directions ➤ Below is a map of Panzozo, a fictitious developing nation in the South Pacific. Panzozo is a showcase for many of the problems addressed in the lesson. Using information from the map, answer the questions that follow.

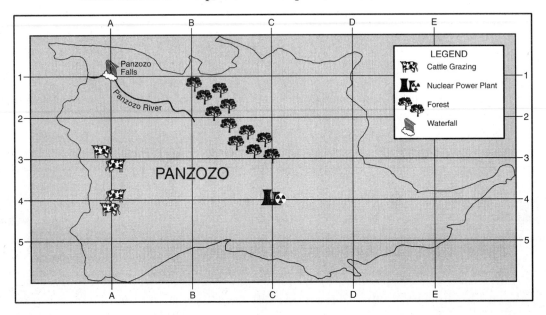

1. Identify by coordinates (that is, by letter and number) the area of Panzozo that is most susceptible to desertification. Explain your answer.

   _____

2. What health threat is posed by the object at coordinate C4? What solution to this problem could you suggest to the Panzozo government?

   _____

   _____

   _____

3. If Panzozo follows the lead of other developing nations in its part of the world, what decision might its leaders make to provide food for its rapidly growing population? What will be the cost of this decision?

   _____

   _____

   _____

ACTIVITY 100 Applying Health Skills

Meet the Burstons

Directions ➤ The following story tells of a typical morning in the Burston household. Read the story. Then, in the space below, tell how each family member is harming the environment and what each could do to clean up his or her act.

"Calvin," Mrs. Burston called up the stairs to her son, "breakfast!"

"Is he still in the shower?" her husband said, looking up from his newspaper. "He's been in there for over half an hour. That boy sure loves to run up my water bill."

"Speaking of water, John, when are you going to fix the leaky faucet in the downstairs bathroom?"

"I'll try to get to it this weekend, Dear," Mr. Burston replied.

Calvin entered the kitchen. "I thought I smelled bacon," he said, eyeing the empty stove top.

"Good morning yourself," said his mother, shaking her head. "The bacon is cooking in the oven. That way I don't get grease all over the kitchen. Sit down and have some juice." She poured the last of the orange juice into his glass and tossed the empty glass bottle in the trash pail.

"How did you sleep, son?" asked Calvin's father.

"OK—once I opened my window to let some cold air in," Calvin replied. "Grandpa keeps the house like a furnace."

"Calvin's right, John," said Mrs. Burston to her husband. "I checked the thermostat first thing this morning, and it was set at 80 degrees. If your father is chilly at night, he should use another blanket."

"I'll speak to him," John Burston said. He looked at his watch. "I better get to the office. Anybody need anything downtown?"

"I could use some shampoo," said Mr. Burston's daughter Clarissa, who had just entered the room. "Any brand is OK as long as it says 'organic' or 'natural' on the label. I want to do my part for conservation."

"You could try turning off a light once in a while," her father responded, grinning. "That would conserve a little more of my hard-earned money."

"Daddy!" Clarissa said.

Mr. Burston waved and left.

"Clarissa, help me set the table," her mother said, handing her the paper napkins.

"At Arnie's house, they use cloth napkins," Calvin said, folding a napkin at each place.

"My, aren't they getting fancy," Mrs. Burston said.

"It's not to be fancy," Calvin responded. "Arnie's mom says it's better for the environment."

Mrs. Burston snuffled. "I have enough laundry to do without washing a load of cloth napkins."

_____

_____

_____

_____

_____

_____

_____

CHAPTER **33** Study Guide

STUDY TIPS
- Read the Health Concepts for each lesson.
- Look up the meanings of any Health Terms that are unfamiliar.
- Read the questions below before you read the chapter.

Directions ➤ As you read the chapter, answer the following questions. Later you can use this guide to review the information in the chapter.

LESSON 1

1. What is air pollution?

_____

_____

2. Explain the sources and the effects of each of the following undesirable gases.

a) Carbon monoxide: _____

_____

_____

b) Hydrocarbons/smog: _____

_____

_____

c) Chlorofluorocarbons: _____

_____

_____

3. Define and give two examples of *particulates*.

_____

4. Why is it important that sewage and industrial wastes dumped into rivers, lakes, and streams be biodegradable?

_____

5. Explain how using pesticides on your lawn can cause water pollution.

_____

_____

6. What is the largest single source of oil pollution in ocean regions?

_____

_____

LESSON 2

7. What is the term for any substances that are explosive, corrosive, flammable, or toxic to human or other life forms?

_____

8. What problem has arisen from the widespread use of nuclear energy by industrialized nations?

_____

9. What is deforestation? What has caused this problem?

_____

_____

_____

10. Define *desertification*.

_____

_____

LESSON 3

11. What is the term for concern about the preservation of the environment?

_____

12. Give one action you can take in your home to conserve energy in each of the following areas.

a) Water: _____

_____

b) Lighting: _____

_____

c) Cooking: _____

13. What are two "dividends" to the environment of recycling?

_____

_____

14. Give recycling guidelines for each of the following materials.

a) Aluminum: _____

b) Cardboard: _____

c) Glass: _____

15. Name two things you can do to protect the environment.

_____

_____

_____

CHAPTER 34 Vocabulary

accident chain	Occupational Safety	blizzard
situation	and Health	vehicular safety
smoke detector	Administration	road rage
fire extinguisher	(OSHA)	date rape
electrocution	hurricane	acquaintance rape
	tornado	

I. Directions ➤ An analogy compares two words or ideas in a way that shows some similarity or relationship between them. An *analogy sentence* is an analogy in which one of the terms is missing and must be inferred. For example, in the analogy sentence *accident is to injury as* _____ *is to safety*, the missing term, *prevention*, might be arrived at using the following logic: "In just the way that accidents can lead to injury, so can prevention lead to safety." Complete each analogy sentence below by writing one of the words or phrases from the above list.

1. hurricane is to rain as _____ is to snow

2. fire is to burn as electricity is to _____

3. chapter is to book as _____ is to accident chain

4. seat belt is to _____ as helmet is to bicycle safety

5. _____ is to windstorm as hurricane is to rainstorm

6. life jacket is to boat as _____ is to home

7. casual friend is to acquaintance rape as boyfriend is to _____

8. _____ is to smoke as motion detector is to movement

II. Directions ➤ Analogy sentences express different relationships such as *cause to effect* or *synonyms* (words having the same or similar meanings). The analogy sentences below contain terms or ideas from the chapter. Complete the sentences using other terms or ideas. Be sure your sentences have the relationship stated in parentheses. The first one is completed for you.

9. rushing is to fall as cigarette is to fire *(cause to effect)*

10. _____ is to natural disaster as road rage is to _____
    (example to category)

11. _____ is to protection as smoke detector is to warning *(object to purpose)*

12. _____ is to date rape as violence is to _____
    (synonyms)

ACTIVITY **101** Applying Health Skills

In Case of Fire

Directions ➤ Each year thousands of lives are lost in home fires. Many of these deaths occur due to a lack of planning and proper prevention. How well prepared is your home and your family? The checklist below will help you answer that question. Complete the checklist, including the escape map. Post the map in a highly visible place in your home, and review it periodically with family members.

Fire Safety Checklist

■ Smoke detector(s) may be found in the following location(s):

_____

■ Last date on which the smoke detector(s) and batteries were tested:

_____

■ Location(s) of fire extinguisher(s):

_____

■ Last date on which pressure dials on fire extinguishers were tested:

_____

■ Location outside of home where family will meet in the event of emergency evacuation:

_____

■ Escape route map:

ACTIVITY **102** Applying Health Skills

Safe at First (and Elm)

Directions ➤ As Municipal Safety Director for Midland City, your job is to deal with threats to the safety of the townspeople. One section of town that has become a particular trouble spot in recent months is the area around the intersection of First and Elm Streets. Read the following complaints passed along to you by the mayor. Identify the safety threat posed by each situation. Then decide what action should be taken.

1. The community swimming pool on Elm near the corner of First was the scene of 38 drowning incidents in the past year. One of the worst accidents occurred when a diver collided with an underwater swimmer. Eyewitnesses claim that if a lifeguard had been on duty, the accident might have been avoided.

    Safety threat: _____

    Action recommended: _____

    _____

    _____

    _____

2. Midland County Hospital has asked for additional funding for emergency room staff. A main cause of the overworked emergency room is the abnormally high number of injuries sustained by workers using outdated equipment at a factory located at the corner of First and Elm.

    Safety threat: _____

    Action recommended: _____

    _____

    _____

    _____

3. Geologists—scientists who study the earth and its makeup—have isolated a geological fault running under First Street just south of Elm. The experts feel that some time in the next year or two, an earth tremor may occur along this fault line. Midland City has never had an earthquake before, and it is unlikely the townspeople will know what to do should disaster strike.

    Safety threat: _____

    Action recommended: _____

    _____

    _____

    _____

ACTIVITY 103   **Applying Health Skills**

Death on Wheels

Directions ➤   For years, safety experts believed that driving over the speed limit was the lone culprit in highway deaths. Recent findings, however, suggest that although speed does kill, other factors play a role in the high number of fatalities on our nation's roads each year. The graph below shows statistics for a recent year. Using information from the graph and the lesson, answer the questions that follow.

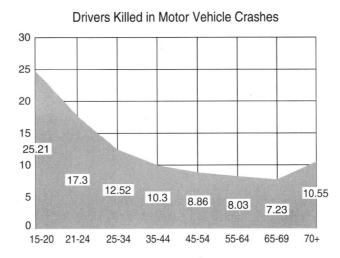

Drivers Killed in Motor Vehicle Crashes

1. In which age group does the greatest number of traffic deaths among drivers occur? What factors might explain these numbers?

_____

_____

_____

2. In what way does the problem addressed in question 1 represent a problem for drivers as well as passengers of all motor vehicles?

_____

_____

_____

3. Do you think the numbers in this graph are limited to automobile drivers? Explain your answer.

_____

_____

_____

4. What strategies can you recommend for reducing all the numbers in the graph, especially the ones at the extreme left?

_____

_____

ACTIVITY 104 **Applying Health Skills**

Thirteenth Precinct

Directions ➤ It is a busy night at the Thirteenth Police Precinct. Below are parts of reports filled out by the desk sergeant. Using information from the reports and the lesson, answer the questions that follow.

A. Thursday, 11:39 P.M. Female, age 27, complained of having been sexually attacked by unknown assailant while walking to her car, which was parked in the Upton Mall parking lot. Victim affirmed she would be unable to ID her attacker because it was too dark in the lot to see his face.

B. Friday, 12:07 A.M. Suspect—male, age 19—brought in for assaulting 16-year-old neighbor. Minor's parents, who were out at the time of the crime, claim suspect forced entry into their home, even though first detective on scene claims back door was unlocked.

C. Friday, 2:12 A.M. Victims—males ages 17 and 18—claim they were taking shortcut through bad part of town. Stopped to help motorist in distress. Were robbed and beaten; failed to get assailants' license plate number or even to identify make and model of car.

1. Identify by letter the report that involved a possible incident of acquaintance rape. What error did the victim in this crime make?

_____

_____

_____

2. At what time did an act of violence involving a deception occur?

_____

_____

_____

3. What preventive behaviors did the victims in the crime mentioned in question 2 fail to exercise?

_____

_____

_____

4. What preventive behavior did the victim of sexual assault fail to exercise? How can you tell?

_____

_____

_____

_____

CHAPTER 35 Vocabulary

first aid	venom	cardiopulmonary
poison	abdominal thrusts	resuscitation (CPR)
pressure point	respiratory failure	xiphoid process
shock	rescue breathing	rabies
poison control center	carotid pulse	gangrene
emetic	cardiovascular failure	

Directions ➤ Use the clues to solve the puzzle. Write one letter of each answer in the space provided. The circled letters will spell out a hidden message about what everyone needs to know how to do in cases of emergency.

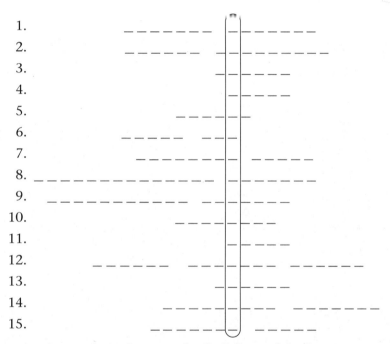

1.
2.
3.
4.
5.
6.
7.
8.
9.
10.
11.
12.
13.
14.
15.

1. Lower part of sternum that projects downward

2. Artificial respiration

3. Any substance that causes injury, illness, or death when introduced into the body

4. Poisonous substance secreted by a snake or other animal

5. Agent that induces vomiting

6. Immediate, temporary care given to an ill or injured person

7. Point along the main artery supplying blood to a limb

8. Failure of the heart to pump blood

9. State in which air is unable to reach the lungs

10. Death of body tissue

11. Failure of the cardiovascular system to keep adequate blood circulating to the vital organs

12. 24-hour hot line providing emergency medical advice on treating poisoning victims

13. Viral disease of the nervous system

14. Application of sudden pressure on a choking victim's diaphragm

15. Heartbeat found on each side of the neck

Hidden message: _____

ACTIVITY 105 Applying Health Skills

When the Pressure Is On

Directions ➤ Knowing how to apply pressure to an open wound can save a life. Do you know how to administer this vital lifesaving technique? Here is your chance to learn. Below is a diagram of the human vascular system, the network of vessels that carry blood to and from the heart. Using outside resources (including your local chapter of the American Red Cross), learn the location of the body's pressure points. Indicate each on the diagram with an X, and draw a line from each X to one of the boxes alongside the diagram. In the box, label the pressure point. Then, in the space provided at the bottom of the page, describe the technique for applying pressure.

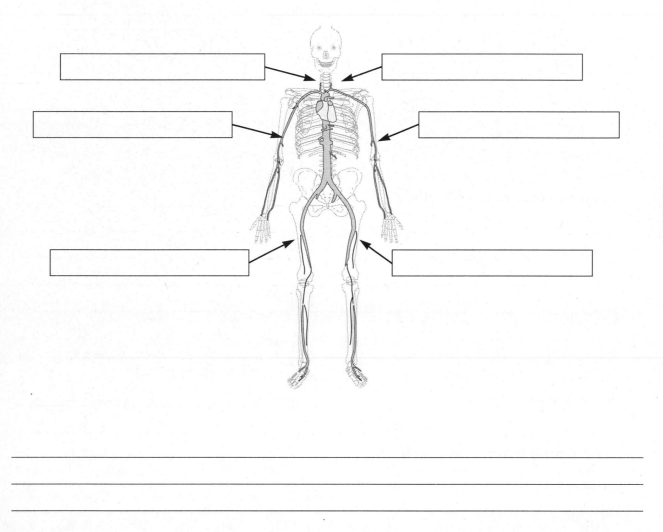

_____

_____

_____

_____

ACTIVITY 106 **Applying Health Skills**

Dial 911

Directions ➤ The following calls have been made to 911. For each call, first decide what questions, if any, still need to be asked in order to have a complete picture of the emergency. Then decide what treatment/procedure should be advised.

1. "I was cleaning the bathroom with this stuff. I knocked the container over, and it spilled all over me. It is burning so bad, I don't know what to do."

   Questions that need to be asked: _____

   _____

   Treatment/procedure advised: _____

   _____

   _____

   _____

2. "My daughter swallowed poison. I went out of the room just for a second, and when I got back I found her. Please help. Should I make her throw up? What should I do? I'm so frightened!"

   Questions that need to be asked: _____

   _____

   Treatment/procedure advised: _____

   _____

   _____

   _____

3. "I was out gardening when this snake crawled out and bit my hand. I put some ice on it so it doesn't swell. There's no one else at home, and I really don't feel very well."

   Questions that need to be asked: _____

   _____

   Treatment/procedure advised: _____

   _____

   _____

   _____

| ACTIVITY **107** | **Applying Health Skills** | FOR USE WITH CHAPTER 35, LESSON 3 |

More 911

Directions ➤ Provide step-by-step instructions for each choking or respiratory failure case below.

1. Toddler was playing near pool when father went into the house to take a phone call. When he went back out, child was lying face down in the water. Child is not breathing.

   Instructions: _____

   _____

   _____

   _____

   _____

   _____

   _____

   _____

2. Woman in restaurant was first thought to be having a heart attack but now appears to have a piece of food lodged in windpipe.

   Instructions: _____

   _____

   _____

   _____

   _____

   _____

   _____

   _____

ACTIVITY 108   **Applying Health Skills**

Safety in Numbers

Directions ➤ An important part of responding to emergencies is knowing where to turn for help. Complete the first form below, and post it in a visible place in your home. Provide additional lines for family members as needed. If you are one of the thousands of teens who make money each year by baby-sitting, make copies of the second form, and fill one out for each child you care for. Be sure to keep the form with you when you sit for that child.

Emergency Numbers

Police: _____

Fire: _____

Ambulance/Rescue Squad:

_____

Hospital Emergency Room:

_____

Poison Control Center: _____

Doctor: _____

Pharmacy: _____

Neighbor, Relative, or Other Adult:

_____

Taxi or Car Service: _____

Family Member 1:

Name: _____

Medicines: _____

Allergies, if any: _____

Family Member 2:

Name: _____

Medicines: _____

Allergies, if any: _____

Family Member 3:

Name: _____

Medicines: _____

Allergies, if any: _____

Family Member 4:

Name: _____

Medicines: _____

Allergies, if any: _____

Baby-sitting Emergency Fact Sheet

Home of: _____

Address: _____

Phone Number: _____

Child's Age: _____

Child's Weight: _____

Medicines Child Takes: _____

Allergies, if any: _____

Emergency Phone Numbers:

Police: _____

Fire: _____

Ambulence/Rescue Squad: _____

Hospital Emergency Room: _____

Poison Control Center: _____

Child's Doctor: _____

Pharmacy: _____

Neighbor, Relative, or Other Adult: _____

Taxi or Car Service: _____

CHAPTER 35 Study Guide

STUDY TIPS
- Read the Health Concepts for each lesson.
- Look up the meanings of any Health Terms that are unfamiliar.
- Read the questions below before you read the chapter.

Directions ➤ As you read the chapter, answer the following questions. Later you can use this guide to review the information in the chapter.

LESSON 1

1. What are the six priorities in an emergency?

_____

_____

_____

2. What are the four types of open wounds?

_____

3. Name the four steps involved in treating any open wound.

_____

_____

4. Briefly describe each of the following types of burns.

a) First-degree: _____

_____

b) Second-degree: _____

_____

c) Third-degree: _____

_____

LESSON 2

5. Define *poison control center.*

_____

_____

6. What is an emetic, and when is it used?

_____

_____

7. What steps should you take if someone comes into contact with a poisonous chemical?

_____

_____

_____

LESSON 3

8. What are abdominal thrusts? By what other name are they known?

_____

_____

9. What technique should be used when respiratory failure occurs?

_____

10. What do the letters *A*, *B*, and *C* stand for in the ABC's of CPR?

_____

11. What is the xiphoid process? What is its role in the administration of CPR?

_____

_____

_____

LESSON 4

12. Explain how to keep a broken bone from moving.

_____

13. What are the three steps of first aid for minor burns?

Step 1: _____

Step 2: _____

Step 3: _____

14. What is gangrene?

_____

_____

15. What is the first thing you would do to help a person suffering from heat cramps?

_____

_____